Writing Is Revision

Arts, Creativities, and Learning Environments in Global Perspectives

Series Editors

Tatiana Chemi (*Aalborg University*)
Anu M. Mitra (*Union Institute & University*)

VOLUME 13

The titles published in this series are listed at *brill.com/acle*

Writing Is Revision

Compositions from the Feminist Fringe

By

Cate McGowan

BRILL

LEIDEN | BOSTON

All chapters in this book have undergone peer review.

The Library of Congress Cataloging-in-Publication Data is available online at https://catalog.loc.gov

Typeface for the Latin, Greek, and Cyrillic scripts: "Brill". See and download: brill.com/brill-typeface.

ISSN 2589-9813
ISBN 978-90-04-71235-5 (paperback)
ISBN 978-90-04-71236-2 (hardback)
ISBN 978-90-04-71237-9 (e-book)
DOI 10.1163/9789004712379

What would happen if one woman told the truth about
her life?
The world would split open.

MURIEL RUKEYSER, "Käthe Kollwitz"

• • •

Don't you think people make a distinction between a story that is
true and a story that is imagined or invented?

SUSAN SONTAG, "Voices: To Tell a Story with John Berger and Susan Sontag"

• • •

I could fill you up with stories,
stories I ain't told nobody yet,
stories with your name, your blood in them.

JO CARSON, "I Am Asking You to Come Back Home"

• •
•

Contents

Acknowledgements

Some of my essays address the paradox of how fiction can also present the truth. The irony does not escape me, then, that I must assure readers I have faithfully rendered the events and experiences in my essays—it all happened. However, I have changed some individuals' names and identifying details to protect their privacy. Though I recall conversations keenly, what I have written does not represent verbatim documentation. Instead, I sometimes recount discussions to capture their tenor and meaning.

PART 1

Strands

∵

The strands are all there: to the memory, nothing is ever really lost.

EUDORA WELTY, *"One Writer's Beginnings"*

∴

CHAPTER 1

What I Mean When I Talk about Women's Lives

I can tell a lot about the owner of a car I am sitting behind as I wait through a long traffic light—for example, the old Ford in front of me yesterday. It was a beat-up 1980s sedan, brown with peeling paint, and its tires were nearly flat. Plastered on the rear window was one of those handmade memorial white stickers with tiny letters and a cross: "In memory of '_____,' who perished in 2012, Afghanistan. Gone home to the Lord." And the car's bumper stickers, scattered all over, were also revealing: "*Semper Fi*," "Elvis is King," "nObama," and "My Other Grandchild is a Chihuahua."

When the light turned green, the car thumped away, and I knew everything I needed to know about that lady behind the wheel—her religious beliefs, political affiliations, pet preferences, musical tastes, financial situation, purchasing habits. Her grief.

I have never slapped stickers on my car, but I often wonder how people might similarly profile me when they meet me, pegging my background, assessing my appearance, and making snap decisions about my socio-economic status and politics. I used to care, but I have grown to care less about what people think as time passes. Instead, I prefer to focus on what matters to me, how I feel about myself, especially my writing. However, I still must put my best foot forward and make an excellent first impression in the opening paragraphs of an essay or book, like here.

In my undergraduate studies, one of the first pieces of feminist art criticism I read was "Why Have There Been No Great Women Artists?" by Linda Nochlin (1971/1988, p. XII). Its "first impression" shifted my way of thinking. It is an influential essay that challenges art history's staid theories (written by men) and questions the institutional barriers that have always prevented women from achieving the same recognition as their male counterparts. It was epiphanic for me—I finally understood why all the women artists in my family had struggled, why I was struggling. Nochlin argues that any so-called absence of "great" women artists is not because women lack talent, but because, historically, society has denied females the same opportunities for education and artistic development. Nochlin's essay sparked a significant shift in the art world in how art historians talked about art, and it also opened the door for more inclusive criticism that values the contributions of women and other marginalized groups.

I have often ruminated about the uphill battles through which other creative females have labored and why this battle touches me personally. My family unfavorably viewed my intellectual pursuits from the start. Because they considered me attractive, my appearance was supposedly my ticket to wealth and happiness. Of course, I disagreed and went to college without emotional or financial support. Once, when I came home for Christmas, I told my family how I struggled to make ends meet a thousand miles away as a full-time student. My grandfather, a moderate business success, responded, "Why don't you just quit and move home? Become a secretary." My mother repeated the same sentiment. Of course, their lack of understanding angered me. It made me that much more stubborn and dedicated to my studies. To this day, I still seek to champion women writers who express my anger about the treatment of females.

Laura Cereta, a Renaissance humanist who lived from 1468 to 1499 and an early voice for women's education and intellectual freedom, presents a compelling argument for women who are interested in higher learning in her "Defense of Liberal Instruction of Women":

> Women have been able by nature to be exceptional, but have chosen lesser goals. For some women are concerned with parting their hair correctly, adorning themselves with lovely dresses, or decorating their fingers with pearls and other gems. Others delight in mouthing carefully composed phrases, indulging in dancing, or managing spoiled puppies. Still, others wish to gaze at lavish banquet tables, to rest in sleep, or, standing at mirrors, to smear their lovely faces. But those in whom a deeper integrity yearns for virtue, restrain from the start their youthful souls, reflect on higher things, harden the body with sobriety and trials, and curb their tongues, open their ears, compose their thoughts in wakeful hours, their minds in contemplation, to letters bonded to righteousness. For knowledge is not given as a gift, but [is gained] with diligence. (1488/1983, p. 83)

By highlighting the societal expectations that divert women's attention from intellectual pursuits to superficial preoccupations, Cereta champions the potential of women to achieve greatness through education and moral fortitude. Her writings not only challenge the gender norms of her time, but also lay the groundwork for future feminist arguments that advocate for the intellectual and creative emancipation of women.

The tension between societal expectations and personal identity is not unlike the challenges women writers faced throughout history, whose works are often subject to a kind of "first impression" that cannot acknowledge the depth of their creativity and the complexity of their narratives. Much like the scrutiny I apply to my world, feminist literary criticism seeks to unearth these deeper layers, move beyond the superficial, and celebrate women authors' nuanced, often revolutionary perspectives.

Just as Laura Cereta argues for a life of virtue and diligence over superficial adornments, feminist critics challenge us to look beyond the conventional "packaging" of women's literature. They invite us to see the resilience, the rebellion, and the profound intellectual and emotional depth that patriarchal interpretations have long obscured. By engaging with the works of women who defy the confinements of their times, writers like Gertrude Stein, Virginia Woolf, María Luisa Bombal, Leonora Carrington, Shirley Jackson, Angela Carter, Lorrie Moore, and Kelly Link, we are not only paying homage to their genius, but also actively participating in dismantling the very stereotypes that seek to diminish their contributions.

In this light, feminist literary criticism becomes a tool for academic analysis and social change. It encourages a re-examination of the "first impressions" of women's literature and challenges us to see the radical, often subversive energy that fuels it. This criticism pushes us to recognize the dual battles women authors fight: against the limitations imposed by their societies and against the constraints of literary tradition itself.

As I reflect on my journey from rebellious disdain for superficial judgments to deep appreciation for the battles fought by women in literature, I see a parallel path. I have learned to reject superficial judgments. I favor a more substantive understanding of others over first impressions. Feminist art and literary criticism should advocate for looking at what goes into a created piece; the surface of a piece is only part of the big picture (pun intended).

In embracing the critical perspective that everyone matters, we honor the legacy of women who have written against the grain and inspire a new generation of marginalized people to write boldly, unbound by the narrow confines of societal expectations. And so, as I continue to navigate the world—both as a critic and as a creator—I carry with me the lessons of feminist literary criticism, a beacon that illuminates the path toward a more inclusive, fair, and profound understanding of literature and life itself.

· · ·

When I write, I am driven to find the answers to the questions that have bothered me for years. *How can I write stories revealing my "truth"? In what ways does my work reveal the challenges faced by women?* When I discuss these far-ranging questions, I consider how to incorporate disparate points into a cohesive whole. But with so many scholarly and creative concepts swimming around in my head, using linear rhetoric is not optimal.

Instead, I choose a different way of writing. In a book like this, one line of inquiry might narrate; another might examine an academic argument or historical topic. The aim is to create something new as I braid strands. What does a braided essay do? It weaves together different stories or ideas, like strands in a braid, to explore a topic from multiple angles, allowing the writer to combine personal experiences, scholarly research, and other narratives to create a layered understanding of the subject.

The alternating movement of braiding, the back and forth, draws out and highlights my topics and themes so a completed work might point toward a significant conclusion. My writing, therefore, becomes more than the sum of its parts. When I weave distinct filaments into a single composition, I also explore the personal and academic and their correlations, if only connecting peripherally, and lace these conceptual cords into a pattern, a braided essay, using the levels of diction at my disposal.

• • •

Much like sections in a plait, a braided essay uses different modes of rhetoric to weave together concepts, exploring topics from multiple angles. This structure allows the writer to layer individual experiences, scholarly research, and snippets of information. I am drawn to the complexity of the form, just as I am drawn to the chaotic energy of being a musician in a rock band. Both forms allow for a blend of rhythms, themes, and perspectives to come together in a fluid, captivating way.

Similarly, playing in a band means collaborating, with each musician contributing their style to create songs combining individual parts. Writing braided essays and playing music with other people both require careful balance and coordination to create something meaningful. One must appease. The two activities allow for introspection and authentic expression.

Years ago, I was also the fearless manager of our band, coordinating every aspect with precision. However, as a petite woman in a male-dominated industry, I faced constant condescension. Burly sound guys at the board often questioned my decisions and expertise, drowning out my voice with their booming shouts over our pounding drums and screeching guitars. "Little lady, you don't know what you're talking about." But I held my ground, using my musical knowledge to demand what my bandmates and I needed on monitors and mixes. I had to play docile to avoid bruising roadies' egos and retribution—a disgruntled sound tech could create a dissonant disaster during a live show.

And then there were the stage managers who would skulk backstage to see me and make unwarranted advances, forcing me to fend them off with a sharp knee when a simple "no" was not enough. It was a constant battle of asserting myself while navigating the fragile egos and desires of others—a compilation of songs and a combination of instruments to create an impactful set list for each performance while navigating a world dominated by men.

I interweave essay structures to merge ideas and create an interconnected intentionality. My work's nonlinearity is intentional. By employing a braided structure, I make a rhetorical foundation to express myself with a non-dominant voice. I assert my right to participate in current conversations about social change, and my fiction and scholarship serve as the mediums through which I make my stand. I present my most authentic self by merging stories and academic writing, but I also straddle interstitial psychic space—my aware-ness of myself and society's constructions of me. The only way to address and dialogue with my various selves is through code-switching, mixing high and low diction so that I can present my life's multiple writing and research modes and my numerous voices to their fullest.

Code-switching in writing is like a DJ seamlessly transitioning between songs at a festival, changing the rhythm and tune, but keeping the crowd (the readers) connected to the event's overarching theme (the text). Just as a DJ curates a journey through music, I, too, navigate the intricate highs and lows of storytelling, confronting the haunting questions that echo across the silence between the tracks.

• • •

I welcome readers to the page in this first chapter by presenting a few terms. Indeed, discourse (any in-depth discussion involving an exchange of ideas) requires considering both objective facts and subjective perspectives for both the writer and reader; this literary contract often reaches beyond an accep-tance of words' meanings and should include consensus and a kinship of pur-pose. While I explore my memories and purpose for writing, I also want to give readers my understanding of women's roles in contemporary society. Many theoretical terms appear in this book, and I will try to use them in context, integrating the concepts within my arguments.

In the fabric of these essays, my identity as a woman is both the weft and warp, the basis from which I approach the world and my arguments. When I discuss feminism, I mean to talk about how the modern world marginalizes women and brings attention to how the contemporary world marginalizes us and unfairly pushes us to the edges of the stage. I want to ensure females' stories and voices are valued just as much as the men at center stage who often get the starring roles.

Conservative pundits and politicians in recent years have amused them-selves by asking prominent folks, especially females, *What is a woman? What is a female?* Requiring people to justify an essentialist stance reinforces the belief that gender differences are natural, fixed, and rooted in biology. An essential-ist viewpoint suggests that all women and men possess distinctive traits and fulfill specific roles, ignoring cultural, social, and individual variations. Those seeking to maintain the patriarchal status quo attempt to affirm societal systems in which men hold more power and authority in most areas of lived experience, from families to workplaces to governments. This system often limits women's roles and rights, treating them as less important than men. The status quo also seeks to delegitimize women's viewpoints and very being.

I want to include all individuals who identify as women. I do not decide who is feminine and who is not. If someone identifies themselves as a woman, it is enough for me. The construct of gender is not rigid; it physically manifests in various capacities. Susan Stryker discusses this concept in her 2017 essay, "Contexts, Concepts, and Terms," stating, "[B]oth gender and sex can be understood in nonbinary ways" (p. 15). Indeed, "[e]veryone has the right to feel they're living their lives in the gender they consider themselves" (Stryker, 2017, p. 14). Language and semiotics play a significant role in constructing our identities; biology is not the only determining factor for how we view ourselves.

Any broader dialogue about identity and expression echoes American philosopher Judith Butler's trailblazing exploration of gender as a performative act. Her ideas laid the groundwork for the other gender critics who followed her, including Stryker, Sara Ahmed, and Lauren Berlant. In Butler's books *Gender Trouble* (1990) and *Bodies That Matter* (1993), she challenges traditional ideas, suggesting gender is not something we possess when we are born, but that gender depends on society's expectations:

> In this sense, what constitutes the fixity of the body, its contours, its movements, will be fully material, but materiality will be rethought as the effect of power, as power's most productive effect. And there will be no way to understand "gender" as a cultural construct which is imposed upon the surface of matter, understood either as "the body" or its given sex. Rather, once "sex" itself is understood in its normativity, the materiality of the body will not be thinkable apart from the materialization of that regulatory norm. "Sex" is thus, not simply what one has, or a static description of what one is: it will be one of the norms by which the "one" becomes viable at all, that which qualifies a body for life within the domain of cultural intelligibility. (1993, p. XII)

Butler illuminates the interplay between societal norms, power dynamics, and individual identity, positing that the very notion of "sex"—often perceived as a natural and unchangeable attribute—is, in fact, deeply entwined with social regulations and expectations. Through this lens, Butler dismantles the conventional gender binary and suggests that the cultural and social frameworks where we exist can shape and reshape our understanding of our bodies and identities. We must rethink the foundations of identity, pushing beyond the traditional boundaries to recognize the performative nature of gender as an ongoing, dynamic process rather than a fixed state of being. In doing so, we must critique the existing structures of power and knowledge and open a space for more fluid and inclusive understandings of identity.

I am not trying to incite confusion with any definition of gender. Instead, I draw my own lines (or, in this case, erase them). In erasing these lines, I step into a space of fluid identities and performances, a realm deeply explored by thinkers like Butler and Stryker, whose works illuminate the intricate identities inherent in gender. Both "woman" and "female" are inclusive terms despite the current lexicographical debate about the term "woman," an unnecessary examination initiated by a male-dominant society that has historically controlled and defined the word.

Yes, in my critical and creative work, I use the words "woman" and "female" to denote the broadest possible range of people. This array includes individuals who identify as females (regardless of assigned gender at birth) and individuals who have at any time been recognized and treated as women (irrespective of current gender). The focus is on limitations and expectations, not understanding womanhood. My writing delves into the experiences of individuals raised as girls and socialized to navigate the world as women. On another equally valid track, sometimes a person's body and presentation invite people to perceive them as female or to respond to them in ways informed by cultural views of femininity. In these cases, too, my stories are written for them; indeed, society might have even more expectations, restrictions, and oppressions for trans women and nonbinary people. I might not directly discuss these subjugations, but I want to acknowledge them.

I do not want to exclude anyone, however. Any person who has ever felt "less than" is welcome. I also hope readers identifying as male may find meaning in my tales. In our patriarchal society, people often insult men by comparing them to women—sometimes, they label them as "too feminine" or "hysterical" when they display anger, sadness, or sensuality. Some men may not even realize that they have been subjected to misogynistic put-downs. My stories should evoke empathy in any reader who has experienced our culture's narrowmindedness. People are outsiders at various points in their lives, and I intend to honor those feelings.

• • •

White Western feminism follows a narrow path through a vast forest. While this dominant feminist perspective offers a route forward, it neglects other trails representing diverse women of distinct cultures, races, and backgrounds. Thus, the power dynamics and bigotry found in feminist circles are a problem, as Pakistani American writer and activist Rafia Zakaria exposes in her book *Against White Feminism: Notes on Disruption* (2021). Zakaria emphasizes women activists' inherited power paradigms:

> [There is] a division between the women who write and speak feminism and the women who live it; the women who have voices versus the women who have experience; the ones who make the theories and policies, and the ones who bear scars and sutures from the fight. (2021, p. 5)

Indeed, feminists must reconsider contemporary female activism and decentralize white women, not seeking "an elimination of white women from feminism," but "an elimination of 'whiteness' from feminism, in the sense that whiteness has been synonymous with domination and with exploitation" (Zakaria, 2021, p. 187). I aim to act as a humble ally, listening and supporting others as I occupy less space as a white woman. Embracing a role of allyship, I turn to the literature that has shaped my understanding, where each story and character are threads in the broader narrative.

Feminism's boundaries also include lines drawn between society's more accepted "others" and society's less accepted "others." Those who are more accepted, the white and middle-class, may work against the interests of the less accepted, anyone Black, Indigenous, Brown, transgender, and indigent. As a working-class woman who has struggled for equity, I also see the vast class disparities and intersections complicating easy categorization. And so, the crucial perspective Zakaria reveals is a distinction between overbearing, professional feminists and those with "lived experience" (2021, p. 7). The divide is not insurmountable, but we must acknowledge that simplifying human relations benefits no one.

As someone who has lived in poverty, I appreciate and endorse that it is necessary to make space at the feminist table for those who are less seen. And I will not appropriate any voice. I am limited to only my perceptions, and I accept the challenge of eliciting change from my point of view.

•••

I seek to change—myself and the world. Looking back at my early critical studies and meandering path, I found models for affecting society in a wellspring of feminine literature. I continue to be inspired. My latest story collection,

Cherry Bomb, which is still in the early draft stages, reflects an accumulation of my literary knowledge. The book comprises woman-themed stories representing alterity as I lean on modernist, postmodernist, and magical realist tropes to question patriarchal hegemony. Thus, my work expresses complex ways of living in a world no one experiences as black and white; it is defiant fiction shirking off the labels that have held me back in the past.

But writing is not my only source of amelioration. Reading literature informs my ideas. Many stories, theorists, and authors have left an indelible mark on my worldview. My favorite types of literature focus on haunted emotions, and I specifically focus on parsing works' metaphysical strains *à propos* to their publication eras' political and social climates. In my writing, I strive to reflect my attention to this slant in literature and inspire revolutionary responses. My investigations of the feminine experience attempt to ground contemporary viewpoints and expand current interpretations of the canon.

Indeed, I take inspiration from those who have preceded me, the many theorists I admire. Walter Benjamin, a German cultural critic and philosopher, has profoundly influenced me. His encyclopedic *The Arcades Project*, an unfinished work written between 1927 and 1940 and translated in the late 1990s, has inspired me for decades as an exemplar of purposeful randomness. When I read the first translations of fragments of *Arcades* in the early 1990s, I realized I was looking at something groundbreaking. It is a stochastic composition at its best. Benjamin's project focuses on the arcades of 19th-century Paris—glass-encased complexes serving as centers of modern consumerism. In *Arcades*, which Benjamin groups into 36 distinct categories with such far-ranging titles as "Fashion," "Boredom," "Photography," "Catacombs," and "Advertising," he provides a patchwork of passages and aphorisms, snippets of published sources and records, and ephemeral and haunting personal impressions: "The first tremors of awakening serve to deepen sleep" (Benjamin, 1999, p. 391). As a Marxist, Benjamin directs his gaze to "the commodification of things" (1999, p. XII)—a change he considers the modern era's most significant development.

• • •

In my writing process, I strive to capture the complexity of humanity and reveal the truths that often go unspoken. This pursuit is rooted in a belief in people's capacity to rise from immanence and overcome challenges. I want my writing to go beyond noticing. I want it to improve conditions and challenge the status quo. Here, my essays about writing craft dissect how I compose, specifically how my fiction attempts to resonate with authentic emotions and elicit genuine reader empathy. I also analyze the intricate nature of female expression. If I can inspire transgressive thoughts in others, I win bonus points. My multi-level studies have enhanced my capacity to create, grounding me with a knowledge base. Through my explorations of other writers' texts with my lens of theoretical ideas, I delve into technical, philosophical, spiritual, and theoretical concepts. Most importantly, in examining my own work and propensities, I have gained a deeper insight into all the concepts shaping my writing.

When I immerse myself in telling a story, it is enthralling. I toss off the yoke of reality and fly. It is like stepping through a portal to a place where the laws of reality bend to the imagination, where I can explore lands unbound by the constraints of science. When creating fictional people who embody subtle themes, I can also discard my psyche and live a different person's life. However, I attempt to create characters who exhibit humanity, unlike any human I know or have ever met. Sometimes, my characters fly, rouse the dead, cavort with wild animals. Or they may not be people at all. But they think like humans. My characters lead me through a tale; they know best, so I travel with them on their often uncomfortable or terrifying journeys to places with quasi-realistic features, but they do not occupy any space we know here on Earth.

None of my short stories are truly autobiographical. Why? Because I fiddle with reality and devise absurd plots. Though I am not a master of the word, I work to provoke readers and ask them to contemplate who they are and why they have made their choices. I have accepted that my efforts are not exemplary by any standard, but I am often satisfied with my drafts when I write with an agenda—I know it is a counter-intuitive strategy. The trick is to permit my narratives to come to me in their own time and not force them—stories arrive when I stay open to memories and hew to my current situation. I begin with an idea to expand upon; for example, what if all males vanished one day? I also self-enforce the mandate in my daily life that I must observe how people act. I aim for truth in emotion while creating unreal settings. The paradox suits me.

My favorite literary topics confront supernatural and psychological hauntings because my past haunts me. People take vacations from their work lives to recharge and reinvigorate, and my fiction functions similarly for me. Drafting stories is a respite—it helps me escape my boring life and tackle my concerns about the challenges women face. By utilizing fantastical elements to reconfigure reality, I model my pieces after the works of female fiction writers who also have grappled with the shifting meanings of women's existence. The authors who most inspire my flights of fancy include Gertrude Stein, Virginia Woolf, María Luisa Bombal, Leonora Carrington, Shirley Jackson, Angela Carter, Lorrie Moore, and Kelly Link, and I will compare my work to theirs later in this book, discussing how each author's style influenced mine.

•••

Revolutionary outlooks in literature can inspire acceptance of divergent views. Indeed, as second-wave feminist Joan Kelly contends in *Women, History, and Theory*, women's viewpoints, their "vantage points," can influence how society accepts separate ways of discerning; highlighting women's perspectives might transform people's understanding of history (1986, p. 8). We all experience the world filtered through our identities. Our unique positions affect our world experiences, a state known as intersectionality that encompasses social identity, race, gender, and class. We stand at a crossroads of multiple paths (identities) influencing our journey (experience). Though I cannot fully understand others' lives, my intersections contribute to my deep empathy for the downtrodden. Yet, my privileged white vantage point has also influenced my perceptions of society, which makes me worry that my feminist protests make me officious.

I must find space in my criticism for feminine writers who challenge a world shaped by men; I must focus on breaking down barricades and dedicating myself to studying authors interested in women's experiences. So, I should rejigger one of my research questions. I should ask, *How do individuals haunted by their pasts create anything when the reality of male hegemony limits their choices?*

• • •

When I write about myself, I reflect on my female experiences under the many umbrellas of oppression. It also means I chase many rabbits off the trail, my artistic endeavors mimicking my stream of consciousness. I am an associative writer. In a 2019 interview, fiction writer Amy Hempel spoke of her own associative writing, her intuitive process of building a story out of various voices and pieces: "There is a leap of faith necessary as thoughts and recollections accrue—you must trust that there is a reason they are occurring when they do. ... Patterns proceed from the accrual" (para. 7). In Hempel's process, as I understand it—and in mine, as I practice it—the writer imposes logical organization and patterns on material, but the writer seldom understands where they are going until they get there. Groping in the shadows is not the sole approach. For writers taking the "leap of faith," we must ask the reader to jump hurdles.

Last year, I drafted an associative story, "You Forgot to Carry the One," with a linear plot. It is still in the fourth-draft stage. In the first draft, I began free-writing, listing objects I still possess from my childhood; all are gifts from friends or discoveries I made when I was a kid in the woods behind my house. I took that list and tried to write a series of associated images. In the second draft, I cut all the objects out except for three Indian coins I received when

I was eight. Soon, a coming-of-age theme revealed itself as I detailed each object's acquisition. But the story is not autobiographical. My omniscient narrator, who is not me, speaks about the protagonist's first crush:

> [H]er mind wandered, inventing conversations, discussions with no more awkward silences on her end, her wit matching his (for once). She traced the memory of his curlicued voice, caressed his smooth syllables intoning about fractals and migrating birds and the golden mean, and she imagined stroking the bridge of his nose, what that would feel like, the black hair at the nape of his neck. (McGowan, 2024, p. 21)

Yes, the distant-sounding narration sets the tone and drives the narrative. If I had employed a first-person narrator or a nonlinear organizational scheme, I would have uncovered another perspective and mood—but it would have been a different story. I make choices that affect the final product at each step of the drafting process. This freedom is the fun of writing.

Readers do not know my process. They only read my final draft, and it is incumbent on them to make associative leaps. I hate making them work, but one of the most fundamental ways to order and interpret confusing experiences is to tell stories. So, I leave a trail of breadcrumbs in my stories, knowing that comprehending and ordering is how sentient beings find safety in a chaotic world. Recognizable patterns and repetition allow one to organize and categorize, to move from the unknowable to something affecting.

My thematic choices often underscore my creations. In my novel, *These Lowly Objects* (2020c), the protagonist, Jules Lalande, lives on different continents, running from authorities—and himself. I did not know where Lalande wanted to go next or where he had been, so I wrote scene after scene to follow him, revealing his involvement in scandals, performances, boxing matches, gritty street scenes, and dozens of relationships. Soon, however, Lalande's maze of travels serves a purpose for the narrative's drive—Lalande's frenetic search for meaning represents his failed pursuits. I order his life's chaos and find a way to the end, discovering a plot as he discovers self-awareness. The assembled pieces, disparate chapters, morph into a complete story of interconnectedness.

• • •

In *The Arcades Project*, Benjamin relays his belief in a profound potential for societal transformation by noticing consumer culture's excess and discards. But understanding excess is not essential for me—creating an experience for the reader matters. Indeed, *Arcades* reads as if Benjamin fashioned a tool for bibliomancy. Open his colossal tome to any page and find him describing Paris, relaying an anecdote, or revealing a factoid: "There is a peculiar voluptuousness in the naming of streets" (Benjamin, 1999, p. 517). For Benjamin, maxims are stepping stones; each revelation is vital to amassing and making sense of life's experiences. His inspiration came from wandering through Paris's once-glistening arcades as a Baudelaire-esque *flâneur* (a walker who observes his urban setting).

When Benjamin interprets Fritz Stahl's impressions of Paris, he observes: "Forming a background to important streets, these buildings give their districts a center of gravity and, at the same time, represent the city as such within them" (1999, p. 526). Every time I delve into *Arcades*, it is like setting off on a journey through the ancient alleys of the old city. Benjamin's accumulated odds and ends provide a center of gravity for the book's overall effect. Similar to the idea that a jaunt through a city is never the same experience twice, every reading of *Arcades* is a new and distinct adventure. I randomly select sections and explore the book's offerings in varied ways with each visit. This dynamic and exploratory approach is what I strive to achieve in my own writing.

Looking at disjointed constructions informs how I address life's random encounters. Besides Benjamin's inspiration, the poet and classicist Anne Carson's work provides fodder for my writing structures. In Carson's 2004 *Paris Review* interview, she reveals, "I like to deal with fragments. Because no matter what the thought would be if it were fully worked out, it would not be as good as the suggestion of a thought the space lends. Nothing fully worked out could be so arresting, spooky" (p. 140). Carson's poetry collection, *Float*, is a physical embodiment of this tack: It is a packet of 22 discrete pamphlets delivered in any order the reader prefers—slide a slender section from the collection stored in a sleeve and begin reading. As the cover touts, "*Float*: A collection of twenty-two chapbooks whose order is unfixed and whose topics are various. Reading can be a freefall" (Carson, 2016).

My drafting process often springboards off my accumulation of unordered fragments, and any of my attempts to make sense of existence only fit the confines of my creations—these fragmented elements might frustrate or inspire readers. Yet we do not have a script for our lives, and we do not organize memories and feelings like folders in a file cabinet (sorry, Anne Carson). Life is a series of associations—thoughts, experiences, emotions, sequential scenes, epiphanies. A person can construe the same moments differently depending on their vantage point.

A singular aim to write inclusive, truth-driven texts is folly, really. Instead, writers must enable readers to impose their own order on the words when they encounter them; the order they choose becomes their story, their truth. We all want to believe someone shares our views, and I try to appeal to readers who recognize something of themselves in my work. I must engage readers in a narrative so they immerse themselves in the story, yes, and perhaps the best way to simulate this verisimilitude is to structure a work with random chronology, letting the reader have an individualized reading experience to organize events for themselves, like how we navigate our lives.

A printed text is static, producing similar reactions for readers because it is the same at each reading. Someday, I hope the "choose your own adventure" method becomes standard. My work is artificial; it is not actual, but I do capture genuine feelings and ideas. In my writing role, there are many ways for me to create valuable gaps in the simulacrum. A more randomized structure forces connections between thoughts, images, or emotions.

Of course, multiple storytelling methods exist, such as the braided essay. Other approaches include Ursula K. Le Guin's "carrier bag theory of fiction" (1986/2019) and the more recently coined hermit-crab story. Le Guin proposed the carrier bag theory as a metaphor, suggesting that stories are like containers of ideas and emotions. Instead of focusing on conflict and heroes, Le Guin's approach emphasizes that storytelling should gather and carry several aspects of human experience, as one might cluster-map overlapping fables. The other storytelling technique, the hermit-crab story, adopts a non-narrative format (like a menu or crossword) to embed a tale. The content "inhabits" the form, much like a hermit crab inhabits salvaged shells, and provides a unique way to explore topics.

• • •

Perhaps, after all, as Roland Barthes conjectures in "The Death of the Author," writers are irrelevant to the text a reader encounters: "[T]o write is, through a prerequisite impersonality ... to reach that point where only language acts, 'performs,' and not 'me'" (1967/1977, p. 143). In a way, Barthes asks writers to imagine a book as a ship launched into the sea of interpretation, and readers are individual captains, steering understanding through oceans of experience only each can chart. After an author launches and publishes a text, readers root through their perspectives' filters to digest the printed words.

When my work is published, I no longer control my words. Barthes based his dead author on Friedrich Nietzsche's warning in the 1880s that "God is dead" in the modern world (1883–1885/2006, p. 5). So, signifying and moving away from authorial authority might democratize literature for the reader and prioritize public perception over elevating creators. And yet, authors are also gods, omniscient and lording over their choices for their texts. I am ambivalent. My ideas clash, and daily, I wrestle with the dilemma of controlling my work or letting go. Navigating the realms of storytelling and reality, my journey through these pages might challenge and expand perceptions, inviting a shared exploration of new truths as I work it out for myself.

If a writer proclaims, *Life is like this*, a reader can only agree or disagree, then decide, *Hey, the author explains life is like this, and I agree (or disagree)*. If I allow readers to discover the truth in the text, they might form their own conclusions. In this journey of discovery, where the lines between writer and reader blur, our shared narratives emerge from the tales I tell and the meanings we weave together when reading. They might say, *I read this book, and it made me think life is like*____. Any truths my reader discovers in the space I make on the page, they will possess and make theirs—and what the reader owns, they treasure.

$$\bullet\ \bullet\ \bullet$$

Readers take a while to understand my associatory writing style. Some of my prose reveals its fragmentary and code-switching origins more than others. I do not sit down with a plan to write a disjointed piece, but it happens because my thoughts often compartmentalize and splinter. My propensity to include different information and emotions reflects how difficult it is for me to face oppression directly. Maybe my radical swings in understanding the roles of an author might foil oppressors. My deflections, nonlinearity, and varied dictions might disarm those who only accept the linear norms they create and promote.

My feminist-themed work attempts amelioration. Can viewing the world from different perspectives *profoundly affect* change? Why would anyone want to read my words? I fear my prose is myopic, strange, and irrelevant. But I will not relinquish the mission I have mandated for myself—it is essential for the tropes I employ to challenge and protest patriarchy. I strive daily to touch the truth in my words. Often, I almost reach validation, writing my essential thoughts. I am careful not to preach. If I have stretched myself and pushed my work into sore places, I have made art that matters to me.

I grieve as I write. It is hard to accept the end of a story I lived in for a while. Writing is akin to accepting mortality. As I write, regardless of how frequently I shuffle paragraphs and reconstitute a work, I cannot delay the inevitable: the cessation of the process and the end of my labor. For this reason, writing is mournful. It also imparts hope and keeps me looking forward to the next page.

References

Barthes, R. (1977). The death of the author (S. Heath, Trans.). In *Image-music-text* (pp. 142–147). Farrar, Straus, and Giroux. (Original work published 1967)

Benjamin, W. (1999). *The arcades project* (H. Eiland and K. McLaughlin, Trans.). Belknap Press of Harvard University Press.

Butler, J. (1990). *Gender trouble: Feminism and the subversion of identity*. Routledge.

Butler, J. (1993). *Bodies that matter: On the discursive limits of sex*. Routledge.

Carson, A. (2004). The art of poetry No. 88. Retrieved March 23, 2024, from https://www.theparisreview.org/interviews/5420/the-art-of-poetry-no-88-anne-carson

Carson, A. (2016). *Float*. Alfred A. Knopf.

Cereta, L. (1983). Defense of liberal instruction of women. In M. L. King & A. Rabil (Eds.), *Her immaculate hand: Selected works by and about the women humanists of Quattrocento Italy* (pp. 81–85). Center for Medieval & Early Renaissance Studies. (Original work published 1488)

Hempel, A. (2019). Amy Hempel on turning survival into a story. Retrieved March 23, 2024, from https://electricliterature.com/amy-hempel-on-turning-survival-into-a-story

Kelly, J. (1986). *Women, history, and theory: The essays of Joan Kelly*. University of Chicago Press.

Le Guin, U. K. (2019). *The carrier bag theory of fiction*. Ignota Books. (Original work published 1986)

McGowan, C. (2020). *These lowly objects*. Gold Wake Press.

McGowan, C. (2024). *Cherry bomb* [Unpublished manuscript].

Nietzsche, F. W. (2006). *Thus spoke Zarathustra: A book for all and none* (A. D. Caro, Trans.). Cambridge University Press. (Original work published 1883–1885)

Nochlin, L. (1988). Why have there been no great women artists? In *Women, art and power and other essays* (pp. 147–158). Westview Press. (Original work published 1971)

Stryker, S. (2017). Contexts, concepts, and terms. In *Transgender history: The roots of today's revolution* (pp. 11–44). Seal Press.

Zakaria, R. (2021). *Against white feminism: Notes on disruption*. W. W. Norton & Company.

CHAPTER 2

Literary Resistance

A novel saved me.

A pivotal moment pushed me to act and choose a different direction for my life. It was a long-ago summer, and I helped a stranger; I will never know if he survived or still breathes.

That year in New York City, I lived with my violent boyfriend, Jesse, whose behavior escalated, moving beyond pushing and slapping in February to punching me in the face in July. Jesse's favorite torture was holding me upside down by my ankles and dangling me off the ledge of our seven-story apartment building. My next-door neighbor called the New York Police Department (NYPD) each time the shouting began, and because they visited often, I got to know a few beat cops by name. Every few days, when I rounded my street corner, I would run into Officer Andretti or Lopez as they moseyed down the sidewalk, and they would holler after me when they saw me sporting a bruised cheek or black eye.

"Hey, there! Where's your old man?"

I seldom saw my boyfriend, Jesse, unless he came home for a change of clothes, and each time he dipped in to see me, the visit escalated to his fist finding my face, slamming the heavy door on the way out, and skipping down the stairs to who knows where. He never said goodbye; he disappeared. I spent my time worrying about how I would pay the rent or afford food if Jesse left for good, though I worked three jobs. When I added them up, my salaries were less than minimum wage—insufficient for an East Village apartment. I was alone, estranged from family and friends—the way Jesse devised to make me depend on him.

It was the hottest summer on record for the Big Apple, and I disconnected from the outside world—no newspaper, no television. But the diner where I waited tables had a TV, and I got my news updates following shows between serving customers. The heat was often the top story, and I enjoyed watching the talk show meteorologists' antics. They would fry steaks or eggs on the sidewalks to prove how blistering it was in the city.

One day, after I worked the early breakfast shift until 10 AM, I headed home toward the subway station, but a crowd blocked my way. A man had collapsed, yet no one helped. I moved closer, recognized the signs of a heart attack, and fell to my knees on the scalding sidewalk to loosen his tie and collar. Without thinking, I leaned in and pressed my lips to the man's dry mouth, counting

© CATE MCGOWAN, 2025 | DOI:10.1163/9789004712379_002

kisses as I inflated his lungs, calculating, imagining my air bubbles traveling down his airway to his lungs, the molecules of oxygen perfect circles like the polka dots on the guy's yellow tie. Every ten breaths, I cupped my hands and compressed above his sternum five times—*one-two-three-four-five*. I repeated the process over and over. Ten exhalations for five pumps. Ten. Five. Ten. Five.

• • •

I have experienced firsthand how my writing has immense potential for harm—a few confessional essays damaged my career and relationships; however, penning my stories has also provided me with a means of expression unavailable elsewhere. Asking, "How does literature have the potential to reveal truths?" is a complicated question. It is the crux of the queries I push myself to answer.

Sadly, the short answer is that literature does not have the direct power to reveal truths about the world or heal anyone's ills, but it can aid people in navigating life's painful journeys and guide readers to ask the right questions so they might enact change in their own lives.

Can literature create change in the world? In my world? In anyone's world? I have attempted to address these questions by studying theory, philosophy, and literary criticism, traveling different roads. Literature straddles a delicate line between personal solace and societal discourse. I find an unexpected counterpoint in literary criticism after the harrowing times I spent in the shadow of Jesse's volatility. Each theory, each philosophical musing on the nature of texts and their impact, echoes how a single novel created a seismic shift in my life. The juxtaposition between the raw chaos of my lived experience and the structured debate of academia underscores a profound truth: literature in myriad forms harbors the power not just to narrate, but to inspire people to alter their lives.

• • •

Two general factions of literary criticism exist. One bloc believes a person should read texts without context because texts are discrete. The other group subscribes to the idea that using literature for palliative care and personal change serves a different function from literature striving for social change. However, any literature melding these two groups' aims, a combined purpose of creating an impression on readers to inspire them to act differently in their lives, is a noble text. It is my goal to write this type of work.

From the dichotomies of literary criticism, I turn to Michel Foucault's examination of texts' intricate dance of power and language, choreography all too familiar in my own life. Much of Foucault's work in *The Archaeology of Language and the Discourse on Language* (1972) examines how and why power structures create texts. Foucault demands rebellious thought, a "structuralism of history," reinforcing how I scrutinize language and search for subtle mechanisms of domination (p. 11). Foucault explains how analyzing the systems enveloping discourse allows us to identify the principles of order, exclusion, and rarity that shape our thinking; institutions enforce these principles to control and minimize individuals (1972, p. 234).

Exclusive language and communication modes hinder inclusivity in the fight against a hegemonic system. Medical nomenclature, for instance, is exclusionary—epidemiologists discuss complex critical health issues in the language of biology and medicine, but laypersons might not comprehend the doctors' meanings because we do not know the terminology. For Foucault, the segregating aspects of language create power structures and barriers that are difficult to tear down. I find echoes of my own literary emancipation in Foucault.

Admittedly, I am not optimistic—an unyielding epistemology drives the damaging residue left by the Enlightenment's worldview. In our fraught times, studying and analyzing social conflicts on all levels is necessary—art and literature provide exposure to concepts inspiring emancipation. Examining society's macro and micro problems and ideas presented in literature is essential to understanding how dominant and damaging power structures impact society. If people learn the methods of resistance through art and literature, they might also enact change. Foucault's dissection of power within discourse lays the groundwork for understanding resistance, not just in grand historical narratives, but in the quiet, everyday acts that shape our existence.

Just as Foucault articulates how discourse shapes reality, literature, in its quiet defiance, offers me a reality reshaped. In the pages of a novel, I discovered rebellion against forced powerlessness and discovered literature's quiet, profound capacity to save; the words threw me a lifeline.

• • •

How does someone resist? James C. Scott, in his essay "Everyday Forms of Resistance" (1989), focuses on operative acts of covert resistance. Contemporary protest movements echo Scott's essay, which directs us toward the notion of effective resistance involving a shared purpose:

> [A]cts [of everyday resistance include] ... foot-dragging, dissimulations, false compliance, feigned ignorance, desertion, pilfering, smuggling, poaching, arson, slander, sabotage, surreptitious assault and murder,

anonymous threats, and so on. These techniques, for the most part quite prosaic, are the ordinary means of class struggle. They are the "first resort" techniques in ordinary historical circumstances in which open defiance is impossible or entails mortal danger. (1989, p. 34)

But who determines if resistance is effective? Those with authority, the ones who chronicle uprisings? Or those who fight and will never read reports of their resistance actions because their movements have been forgotten in the mists of time? How can one enact change if one is not writing one's history? Indeed, observing how victors write the histories of civilizations may be a cliché, but the winners who write accounts conceal reports of the powerless. Yet, literature does not provide a historical record and can, therefore, play a role in avoiding information embargoes, enabling individuals to produce accounts not otherwise recorded for posterity.

Resistance theories resonate with me as I push back against the confines of my circumstances, my efforts finding their way into the stories I pen. As a resister, I understand how important it is to share my activities. Yes, my resistance is a transformative process in my life. Anger affects my impetus to change, but aggression is not the answer. Instead, constructive rage fuels my actions. One of the first stories I wrote in my early years reflects my ire—the ironically titled "Lie to Yourself," which appeared in my first book, *True Places Never Are* (2015). The piece grapples with an individual's power to change their circumstances only after facing life's brutal truths. My second-person narrator experiences a life of chaos when she enacts everyday resistance and has no proper way or understanding of how to direct her desire for change:

> It's easy to wreck your life. Really. Just lie to yourself. No, that's too easy. To wreck your life, to start out with, you should ignore your bills. Or better yet—oh, yes—make an effort to mess things up! Lick stamps with all the wrong outgoing postage and slap them on all your bills with misprinted return labels so your payments won't get to where they're going, so they go to the dead letter office. Nothing gets paid. So, when the phone's cut off, and your temp agency can't reach you, and the trailer rent comes due, and you don't get that paycheck, and you're getting kicked out, you'll only have $1.33 in your bank account. (McGowan, 2015a, p. 189)

The story spirals further into desperate straits until it ends with the narrator living in more dire circumstances, and she cannot escape.

In his essay, Scott distinguishes how repressed transcripts differ from authoritative ones, noting how accepted stories often defer to the rich, educated, and powerful:

> Descriptions and analyses of open political action dominate accounts
> of political conflict. ... The undeniable advances made along these
> lines, however, are fatally compromised by a damagingly narrow and
> poverty-stricken view of political action. There is a vast realm of politi-
> cal action ... that is almost habitually overlooked. ... and ... any account
> which ignores them is often ignoring the most vital means by which
> lower classes manifest their political interests. (1989, p. 33)

While I appreciate Scott's arguments about "peasant resistance," he limits the
nature of revolution to class distinctions. Scott posits how class consciousness is a social construction rooted in reductionism, relegating peasants (and
subordinate classes) to resistance status because they must recognize and
accept their positions as inferiors in social structures. This narrow view of
class is wildly inaccurate. Ironically, Scott authored his essay during a time of
retrenched conservatism in the United States—much of what he writes corre-
sponds to the conditions of the 1980s.

In their essay, "Dispersed Resistance: Unpacking the Spectrum and Properties of Glaring and Everyday Resistance" (2018), critics Mona Lilja and Stellan
Vinthagen continue where Scott leaves off. They supply a more expansive view,
allowing for subtle revolt against dominant institutions and governments.
Understanding social resistance through a Foucauldian lens, Lilja and Vinthagen argue how oppositional forces might threaten an institution from the
inside *and* outside and how dispersed resistance includes enacting everyday
resistance and overt and covert forms of transgression. The two authors explain
more paradigms: "productive resistance" and "counter-repressive resistance"
(Lilja & Vinthagen, 2018, p. 212); to resist, one must assemble tailored responses
in context and toward repressive assemblages of power. My literature attempts
to do just this with its adapted reactions to oppression and repression.

As I discuss the subtle art of resistance, I am reminded of literature's
possibility to inspire quiet defiance. In my own life, each page turned, each
story unfolded, becomes a personal reclamation of space and identity. Literature, with its unassuming power, is my sanctuary, a space where reading is
both an escape and a return to myself. This realization that literature might
save me anchors my narratives and scholarly explorations, bridging the personal and the academic in a testament to the written word's transformative
potential.

•••

The travails of my earlier years have informed the range and breadth of my
writing.

Thus, it is preferable to endorse a less damaging form of struggle in literature and the arts, especially when the social order's stability is as tenuous (if not more so) as in earlier decades. In "Lie to Yourself," the narrator tries to rebel against the "system," but only injures herself. So often, in the act of rebellion, my actions have backfired.

As literary critic Karsten Piep notes, creative expression can be an act of protest as literature can be "an artistic reflection of historical realities ... a socially symbolic act. ... a way of doing something in the world" (2009, p. 7). By reading and writing, people may discover what they think about their social positions and explore alternative perspectives, finding coping mechanisms to address their human experiences.

Reading and composing have also nudged me toward change in my own life. Writing has ruined and rescued me, producing opportunities I would have missed otherwise. I work out complex critical problems on the page and share those insights. Does fiction have a broader impact on people beyond individuals or small communities? I am not so sure. Though skeptical that broad societal change is possible through my stories or verse, I aspire to inspire change, nonetheless. One person at a time.

•••

A braided essay is this essay. Many cultures have traditionally relegated braiding to women who plait each other's hair or work at their looms kept at home. Society views braiding as women's work, even though categorizing such a task as either masculine or feminine is reductive. My women's work of braiding differs from this physical task, but I appreciate the metaphor: I collect threads of stories and meaning from experiences as I interlace them with nonlinear explanations. I code-switch. I braid.

In braided essays, to assist readers in distinguishing one strand from another, writers often add "white space," a visual break in their prose between fragments. White space creates a rhetorical shift, and asterisks between sections indicate that the white space falls between pages. Asterisks in a long poem cue a new stanza appearing on the subsequent page. In my work, I include many space breaks where I pause, providing a respite from intense revelations or breaking up a long passage. These interruptions also show how my thoughts travel on different paths, yet aim at the same destination, connected not by paragraphs, but by theme.

The structure I use for my scholarly personal narratives (SPN) provides a framework for a complex brocade; these essays allow me to merge narratives, demonstrate scholarship, and amalgamate linear and nonlinear forms, personal stories, and knowledge inquiry. By writing a tapestry of stories, I can provide a more comprehensive understanding of my ideas and present moments to any audience receptive to alternative forms of discussion about research. My essays allow me to draw outside the lines and devise new ones to push boundaries. What appeals to me most is that my SPN s enable me to challenge scholarly and creative theories and combine them into novel forms.

• • •

I have alternated between assorted language styles as an author and a woman. When I braid my code-switched experiences, I am rewarded with a deeper understanding of how my ideas connect and how deviation from the "accepted" mainstream way of writing is rewarding. Conventional outlets and people have seldom accepted my language, yet exclusion does not bother me; I have lived on the fringe all my life.

Chicana activist, teacher, and author Gloria Anzaldúa's works introduced me to the formal term "code-switching," the way I have communicated since childhood. It is now a relief to label my diction. I code-switch in most of my writing, using interwoven essay structures and layering stories to tell SPN s; I code-switch to contextualize how and why I write my fiction, yet I must accept I must work on multiple levels with less-than-ideal outcomes.

Because I am an outsider, Anzaldúa's work speaks to me. She seeks ways to rectify language's power to distance as she calls for an understanding and acceptance of all kinds of speech. Anzaldúa validates my views when she defends the silenced and excluded: "Before the words escape our mouths, the real issues [are] ... blanked out" (2009, p. 116). Her arguments glimmer with power as she weaves anecdotes through her pieces and uses the rhetorical ploy of appealing to pathos. Anzaldúa posits how unacceptable it is for any environment to require people to conform to society's mores and eschew their native tongue. Anzaldúa echoes Foucault's theories of language, exclusion, and appropriation, confirming his concepts of verbal barriers in society shaping our circumstances.

A person's speech and writing *are* their identity. We weave communication into our being, and the design is complex, rife with linguistic variables. Thus, my objective is to focus on inclusion rather than exclusion, presenting an extensive integration of ideas and styles—my Southern upbringing and breaking free from strictures, my Irish gift of the gab "chasing rabbits," and my intensive critical theory background.

• • •

Writing is a conversation—I talk to readers by forcing myself to articulate and communicate ideas and secrets I will not vocalize face to face. In staking a multifarious linguistic stance, I straddle two worlds: academia and publishing. However, my choice of structure, the braided essay, is only one aspect of my composition process. My other rhetorical form of choice is the SPN. An SPN is a more complex, individual way of presenting research than traditional academic papers that pose arguments and prove theses using third-person points of view and persuasive rhetoric. Instead of employing a disembodied voice, an SPN, as the name states, centers on a researcher's first-person explications. I use the SPN to present my criticism from a valid scholarly perspective. My fragmented SPN s, which are only pieces of complete narratives, transcend academic or artistic frameworks and engage an audience in my process.

Robert Nash, who popularized the SPN in his book *Liberating Scholarly Writing: The Power of Personal Narrative* (2004), argues for myriad possibilities of hybridizing imaginative and analytical work. My output spans these countless possibilities. I am a third-person rhetorician who researches and culls sources to prove an argument in scholarly language. I am a first-person memoirist who writes in the conversational diction of how I speak as I reveal personal truths that are sometimes difficult to divulge. I am a first-, second-, or third-person poet who inhabits a moment of my own or someone else's and attempts to express the ineffable in a relatable way. I am a first-, second-, or third-person storyteller who uses all the approaches of an academic, memoirist, and poet, moving fluidly across genres to express the human experience of a fictional character because none of my fiction's information is really autobiographical (that is a lie; all work is autobiographical, but I can present untruths as a fiction writer).

The way I understand the SPN's purpose is that it permits an author to write across genres, allowing them to "use their personae in order to explore subject matter other than themselves" (Nash, 2004, p. 28). Yes, even creative writers use composition and research as vehicles for discourse and often bestride various fields to express their unique authorial perspectives. The SPN is dialogic work with scholarly and personal voices balancing on a tightwire.

• • •

How did I go from dark days in my twenties, feeling lost and unsure of my place, to believing literature can drive personal change? I changed my perspective. Or, instead, literature changed me. As a poet, fiction writer, and academic, I have learned to trapeze between modes, conveying and making meaning. On the safe academic platform, I present arguments using source material and evidence to support a thesis before grabbing the trapeze fly bar to soar. Safety and stability are on the circus ring floor, but I aspire to fling myself skyward, hanging in the air, taking creative chances, conveying abstract concepts as concrete, using examples, anecdotes, and narratives. I tell revealing stories about my life, a triple-twisting-quadruple-flip viewpoint, flailing without a net for safety.

When I fuse benign and perilous ways of presentation, I execute complex skills. But I do not stick on the landing most days. How can one take risks while remaining safe? I do not know. While I hazard my work in the most subtle ways, I draw inspiration from women who paved the way for me and faced grave danger—I borrow their methods and perspectives to build my own.

• • •

I sometimes cannot shake my sadness about that distant summer in New York, and I composed a poem about it: "The Lives I Save Are Never My Own" (McGowan, 2019d). When I attempted to adapt my verse to prose (an exercise I often deploy for creating new work), I was unsuccessful—my paragraphs could not adequately express my poem's stanzas' emotional weight. The poem captures my feelings well, but I also acknowledge the need to work through those events by writing them in prose here.

Much as my poetry takes up the emotional slack for my prose, my critical work fulfills a distinct purpose; the two spheres, however, are often at odds. While I aim to convey material reality in my criticism, I choose to author stories that are fabulist by nature, many with a tip of the hat to the last century's narratological ideas. Yet I do not gloss over immanence for women or others in society or attempt to assuage under false cover. Gender and class bigotry have limited my success and well-being, and so I feature neglected female voices and experiences, representations that allow me to subvert and disrupt dominant patriarchal narratives.

As a practicing writer, a woman in the fight, I am dubious about how words can change conditions on a large scale. I suspect literary works hold value for the producer (me), but may not make any impression on readers or culture. Literature includes neither autonomous, transcendent objects nor mere by-products of historical circumstances. Instead, literature might coalesce elements to inspire readers to enact agency or autonomy. I do not wholly believe literature inspires change, a view many literary critics harbor. Though I may not "heal" someone with my writing, I may spur them to consider their lives and circumstances.

Alas, writing to change minds through literature is futile. I embrace this Sisyphean task daily, even with writing's discouraging uphill climb. I am realistic, too, as history is repeating itself—after significant gains in civil rights, the rock of progress is rolling back down the mountain. Literature might make a trivial difference, yet I still dedicate myself to expressing protest and exposing wrongs; this vigilance is my contribution to the fight. In this reflective space, I find not just closure, but also a beginning. The questions posed by my engagement with literature and theory do not demand definitive answers; they invite exploration. Can literature truly inspire change? Perhaps the answer lies not in the grand gestures of social transformation, but in the quiet revolutions of the heart and mind. In authoring this essay, I have navigated my past and charted a course for the future where writing might be an act of resistance.

• • •

The oppressive heat of that long-ago summer in New York City only highlighted how trapped I felt, a metaphor that did not escape me, and I sought refuge in words when I was not working. I escaped into the local library's air-conditioned stacks, a dark haven where I read *Oldest Living Confederate Widow Tells All* by Allan Gurganus (1989). That book changed how I saw my past and present as the protagonist, Lucy Marsden, was living in an abusive relationship like mine. In the Civil War South, Lucy escapes her racist husband and learns it takes action and courage to bring about change. I realized that a person cannot wish for change; to support others requires courage, especially if it means taking a stand against popular opinion. In that book, I found not just an escape, but a reflection of my tangled reality, circumstances that made me almost unable to survive that sweltering summer.

My epiphany unfolded within the quiet confines of a library as Gurganus's narrative echoed my struggles. It was a stark reminder of literature's capacity to not only lay bare our deepest tribulations, but also illuminate that there was a way out of abusive situations. In Lucy Marsden's story, I found not just solace; I discovered a call to action guiding me toward the possibility of emancipation. This catalyzing quality is the essence of literature's silent power to console and confront, to elicit change.

Gurganus's book changed my life.

After I kneeled to help the man on the sidewalk, after I performed many rounds of CPR, he roused and gagged, regurgitated. I pulled back, and his milky, confused eyes searched my face for answers. Without saying a word, I righted his silk pocket square, slid my hand between his shoulder blades, and helped him sit. The crowd erupted in applause, but I hurried away, embarrassed by my stained and sweaty uniform. A distant siren wailed in the background as I descended into the subway station to catch my downtown local. I do not know if the heart-attack man survived. I made it, but I am not sure he did.

References

Anzaldua, G. (2009). *The Gloria Anzaldúa reader* (A. L. Keating, Ed.). Duke University Press.

Foucault, M. (1972). *The archaeology of knowledge and the discourse on language* (A. M. S. Smith, Trans.). Pantheon.

Gurganus, A. (1989). *Oldest living Confederate widow tells all*. Vintage Books.

Lilja, M., & Vinthagen, S. (2018, May 4). Dispersed resistance: Unpacking the spectrum and properties of glaring and everyday resistance. *Journal of Political Power, 11*(2), 211–229. https://doi.org/10.1080/2158379X.2018.1478642

McGowan, C. (2015). *True places never are*. Moon City Press.

McGowan, C. (2019). The lives I save are never my own. *Coal Hill Review*.

Nash, R. J. (2004). *Liberating scholarly writing: The power of personal narrative*. Teachers College Press.

Piep, K. (2009). *Embattled home fronts: Domestic politics and the American novel of World War I*. Rodopi.

Scott, J. C. (1989, May 5). Everyday forms of resistance. *The Copenhagen Journal of Asian Studies, 4*(89), 33–62. https://doi.org/10.22439/cjas.v4i1.1765

CHAPTER 3

A Fight for Truth

I have often heard people differentiate between types of writers: "Fiction writers share lies; poets reveal innermost truths." Such blanket characterizations about authors and their genres reveal what the cultural *Zeitgeist* cheekily accepts as some pseudo-authorial mandate. As a member of different intellectual and artistic communities, I am friends with authors of many stripes, and I have observed how some literati pit poets against fiction writers, purporting that those who write verse reveal the world's truths. Prose writers merely tell stories. Yes, I have often had my word doubted when someone finds out I write fiction.

A while ago, I told a story at a cocktail party, my friends laughing and enjoying my yarn—except for the poet, a laureate, no less, who sat stone-faced in the corner while I regaled the group. After swilling a few more glasses of wine, he sidled over and slurred in his surliest brogue, "Darlin' Cate, you're a fiction writer. Don't ever be a fiction talker." The room fell quiet; my face lost its color. I did not speak again that night.

Poets indeed grapple with emotional truths, often confessing their pain in the verses they compose, and some critics even consider poetry nonfiction. A few astute readers might even believe poems reach objective certainty for the piece's writer. However, I rarely subscribe to this view—my poems often feature speakers who are not me. Do not discount fiction writers; they, too, examine honest feelings and realities, but in a different way. My stories reveal more actuality than my poems; my fiction sweeps across the double veneers of authenticity and fabrication.

When I write anything, poems, prose, or copy for advertising (as I have been wont to do), I consider the cultural connections between truth and language, studying how various approaches to literature and my writing might be at odds with not just seeing the world, but comprehending and understanding it. Hopefully, my approach opens others' minds and directs attention toward others who deserve or need empathy. Though my fiction is autobiographical in its basis, it differs from autobiography. In early drafts of *Cherry Bomb*, I have tried to lend all my protagonists or narrators my name. Still, it read too gimmicky, a danger writers encounter when attempting to employ postmodernist tropes. My characters may not share my name, but they might live through the same events, scenes, and, most importantly, the emotions I have experienced.

© CATE MCGOWAN, 2025 | DOI:10.1163/9789004712379_003

My tales represent my fundamental truths, hopes, fears, and limitations. Petty observations. Sadnesses. Remarkable successes.

• • •

As in all fiction, narrative truth is distinct from factual history or biography. But narrative veracity *is* an emotional truth. In Tim O'Brien's short story, "How to Tell a True War Story," from his collection *The Things They Carried* (1990), the narrator argues that truth does not have to reflect reality. O'Brien's narrator explains the paradox of telling a fictional story, in his case, a war story. The narrator claims, "[A] true war story does not depend upon ... truth. *Happeningness* is irrelevant. A thing may happen and be a total lie; another thing may not happen and be truer than the truth" (O'Brien, 1990, p. 83). *Happeningness* does not matter in my narratives, either. Certain events in a story are intense, and they create a stronger sense of authenticity than reality can. Indeed, fiction can be more truthful than truth.

However, truth is a challenging goal to attain in fiction. My process of asking questions about other people's perceptions and assumptions is critical to positioning myself in scholarly literary conversations and seeking veracity; my critical eye provides me with nuanced stances. There are unusual ways to perceive genuineness. My assumptions about authenticity and perspectives about many facets of scholarship, including objectivities, subjectivities, context, meaning-making, power, critics' positions, and linguistic theory, affect my research design. Cultural connections and underlying assumptions color what I write.

There is no absolute truth, with a capital T, of course. The laws of science, including the inescapable nature of gravity, are not up for debate. But why should I not violate Newton's laws in my fiction? I can create a world with its own sets of rules and regulations and physical laws. My tales present grand reckonings to reveal conditional laws; my stories often feature historical people or factual events coinciding with the lives of my created characters—I write *roman-à-clefs* and fashion lives. And I tweak moral codes and dictate behavior; I ruin relationships; I employ words to reify emotions. Because my real-life experiences are impossible to convey, I most enjoy writing when confronting foreign feelings and innovative ideas germinating in my imagination. I dig in and surprise myself, groping for the truth for both the reader and me. Though I cannot dictate readerly reactions, I fertilize a story's kernels with emotional honesty, especially if a story's elements are too outrageous to mimic real life.

In literature, truth is relative—this is what I am trying to express. As Susan Sontag notes, stories are different enterprises in different contexts:

> [T]here is a kind of ambiguity in the very notion of storytelling. On the one hand, we consider storytelling as a truth-telling activity—"Tell me the real story." Stories bring information. Stories reveal secrets, true stories that might be told after someone's death. Because, for instance, the death of someone is generally an occasion for telling stories about a person's life, and maybe, the truth comes out that wasn't discussed or generally shared before that person was gone. But we also think of stories as, "That's only a story." Or, "Don't tell me stories," meaning, "Don't tell me lies." (Berger et al., 1983, 4:50–5:30)

Sontag describes how I have used my writing to tell both truth and lies. When my stories' plots hinge on untruths, my characters lie to themselves and others, and these prevarications are the basis of my tales' conflicts. Literary veracity is the product of manipulated language, and literary scholars, thinkers, and philosophers should stop professing (or pretending) that there is a singular truth for all people. We must dismantle feeble essentialist assumptions and support acceptable multivalent conceptions of veracity.

The untruths I present in my fiction do not signify my eschewing a belief in the concept of absolute truth—a term encompassing authenticity, a sense of right with no ambiguity; on the contrary, my shady characters and fantastical settings expand the grounds of validity in the unreal worlds I create. One must examine logic and rhetoric to understand the word "ground" in this context. Assumptions inform the term as explained in the Toulmin Method, a rhetorical style philosopher Stephen E. Toulmin devised in his 1958 book *The Uses of Argument*.

In his process, Toulmin notes that each spoken or written argument comprises three essential components: a claim, the grounds, and warrants. The claim is the initial assertion a person tries to prove. The grounds are facts or evidence providing support to the claim. Finally, the warrants connect the grounds to the claim, which can be as simple as stating how one fact leads to another or how specific points are related (Toulmin, 2003). Charles W. Kneupper explains Toulmin's ideas in "Teaching Argument: An Introduction to the Toulmin Model" (1978), pointing out how people assert opinions they want to prove in real life, such as lawsuits. Kneupper also clarifies Toulmin's terms based on their applications. In fiction, a claim might include aspects of a story's theme. In scholarly work, a claim is a thesis researchers must substantiate with evidence; an argument's grounds present the evidence and empirical facts to back the claim; implicit or explicit warrants work to bolster the grounds and assume a link to the grounds' proof of the claim (Kneupper, 1978, p. 237).

Thus, grounds are the basis for expansive thought, using concrete methods to explain how to solve a problem. In *A Grammar of Motives* (1945), literary critic and philosopher Kenneth Burke explores the meanings of grounds (among many other rhetorical devices) and contends that both concrete and abstract usages of *ground* describe motives; he explains the real-life conditions of an argument's grounds: "'On what grounds did he do this?' translates to 'What kind of scene did he say it was that called for such an act?'" (1969, p. 1002). Through my storytelling, I strive to present real-life grounds, offering context to the reader. By exploiting and countering verisimilitude and its grounds, I subvert reality and present a more significant stance—emotional truth.

• • •

When I invent fictional people, those folks inhabit domains of emotional truth even if their worlds differ from what humans encounter on "real" Earth. I depict, yet skew, the circumstances of my milieu. In particular, I populate my fiction with women down on their luck. I can relate. The settings where these women live are the grounds for their actions, interactions, choices, and thoughts. But if I use my experiences to inhabit these stories with my truth, my truth is not the reader's.

As the critic Sissela Bok argues in *Lying: Moral Choice in Public and Private Life* (1989), the dual parts of honesty and moral integrity in literature are symbiotic, but are not interchangeable (p. 6). Words can change hearts and minds, but Bok contends this authority goes beyond storytelling's traditional mandate in which past oral traditions recorded stories and presented a veneer of historical truth, maintaining a narrative's integrity for future generations. In the past, too, the gravitas of a spoken story lent it credibility (Bok, 1989, p. 5). Bok also reasons that many ancient cultures considered art valid and relevant to real life (1989, p. 5). Indeed, Plato's ideals reinforced societies' ethics and posited that opposing truth is undesirable and should be avoided (Bok, 1989, p. 5). Thus, honesty became a default moral choice, especially in art.

Veracity standards have changed in modern cultures, driven by moral choices rather than survival. Society invented the constructs, making candor necessary to address and accept multiple or at odds viewpoints. In modern times, any morality of truth is not determined by whether a person shares a false statement, but if they intend to mislead others (Bok, 1989, p. 6). Bok's arguments emphasize the central intention of my fictional forays—I do not want to share falsities. I write characters who are going through trouble.

The paradox of my fiction's untruths is that my characters and narrators intend to mislead others in their worlds; their dishonesty forces readers to reconstitute their own deeply held notions of certainty. I hope to give readers free rein to discover and identify characters' deceptions, which often develop or stem from coping in a male-dominated world; however, I try not to force any epiphanies. Many of my charlatans and con women live sad lives, suffering the consequences of their own trickery or malicious acts, but my well-meaning characters fib, too. Regardless of how good or bad a character is, I ground their untruths with context—I create happenings in which there are no black-and-white choices between right and wrong. Nuance is necessary. Often, characters must make ambiguous moral choices for self-preservation. In my created worlds, lying sometimes does not repudiate truth; it bolsters it. At the least, prevarications might reinforce a reader's understanding of why people commit evil acts. This reader's realization of the characters' wrongdoings imbues empathy and compassion.

I base my fictional societies and their ills on the literature I admire, such as the allegorical world presented in the novel *Gulliver's Travels* by Jonathan Swift (1726). In one of Gulliver's later voyages, he encounters the Houyhnhnms, a species of intelligent horses who do not understand dishonesty; in fact, no comparable word for *lying* exists in the horses' dominion. When Gulliver explains the concept of telling a lie, the Houyhnhnms mock the idea as a condition of "say(ing) the thing which was not" (Swift, 1726/2005, p. 166). Indeed, the Houyhnhnms cannot comprehend the concept of untruth. I do not have the same problem—I understand what lying means and how destructive a character's fibs and fabrications can be. Hence, events and scenes in my stories often center on the prevarications to underscore my *leitmotifs*. As my narrator in "Bandit, Bank Robber, Thief" declares, the lies they write, "any words you scribble could fill this moment, this twilight absence, this half-moon draining like a bowl" (McGowan, 2024). My themes interrogate current societal assumptions of truth and challenge readers to consider alternative or uncomfortable viewpoints, encouraging those readers to take meaningful stock of their values.

In his book, *The Dialogic Imagination* (1934–1935), twentieth-century theorist Mikhail Mikhailovich Bakhtin explains why a novelist's endeavors differ from a poet's. Bakhtin believes novels decentralize expression and present "a Galilean perception of language, one that denies the absolutism of a single and unitary language—that is, that refuses to acknowledge its own language as the sole verbal and semantic center of the ideological world" (1934–1935/1981, p. 366). Bakhtin also posits novelists "ventriloquate" and "orchestrate" (1934–1935/1981, p. 300), allowing a "multiplicity of social voices and a wide variety of their links and interrelationships (always more or less dialogized)" (1934–1935/1981, p.

264). Many short stories operate as dialogues with the reader and society, and such different points of view may affect a reader's empathy and her ability to observe the world from various perspectives.

Coining the term *heteroglossia*, Bakhtin also contends that a cacophony of voices and motivations in novels is preferable (1934–1935/1981, p. 278). Many languages might dialogize in a work of fiction and are "equally capable of being 'languages of truth,' but since such is the case, all ... are equally relative, reified, and limited, as they are the languages of social groups, professions, and other cross-sections of everyday life" (Bakhtin, 1934–1935/1981, p. 367). Indeed, no singular expression captures the complete picture of a person's experience. All languages limit their speakers and writers' ability to explain what it means to be alive.

In his introduction to Bakhtin's *Dialogic*, the editor and critic Michael Holquist claims Bakhtin's theories about fiction reduce "all plots to two people talking in a particular context" (1981, p. XIX). People interact with tension in real life, and conflicts manifest in culture and discourse; Bakhtin notes that a person's "living utterance" derives meaning in "a particular historical moment in a socially specific environment" (1934–1935/1981, p. 276). Contextual consideration reflects a language's past significance and current use in social and personal interactions. Nonetheless, tension "unfolds" under the aegis of "social *heteroglossia*, ... the Tower-of-Babel's mixing of languages" (Bakhtin, 1934–1935/1981, p. 278). Thus, fiction writers must make their ideas resound above dissonant, irrelevant voices.

My awareness of language's power comes from my need to awaken social awareness and express myself. I want to understand people. Veracity emerges in conversations between characters, but honesty is not absolute. As Bakhtin notes, novels are not soliloquies or monologues; they are nets of navigable relationships, "spring[s] of dialogism that never run ... dry" (1934–1935/1981, p. 330). The heteroglot novel doubts any language-asserting authority as the ultimate expresser of truth; considering absoluteness a gross presumption, Bakhtin calls this the "lie of pathos" (Bakhtin, 1934–1935/1981, p. 401). Polyphonic fiction pits a "lie of pathos" against "a gay and intelligent deception, a lie justified because it's directed precisely to liars" (Bakhtin, 1934–1935/1981, p. 401). For Bakhtin, people are liars, and authorial intention redeems fictional untruths—there are degrees and conditions of falsity in *heteroglossia*.

However, literary creators and critics are not the only scholars who embrace the paradoxical view of fiction presenting the truth. For the contemporary philosopher Richard Rorty, who wrote "Redemption from Egotism" late in his career in 2010, the novel "attempts to put us in relations to persons which are not mediated by questions of truth" (p. 393). Rorty argues that literature aims to find the truth in a democracy; it is a supreme vehicle for moral reflection, more so than philosophy or religion. In an earlier work, *Contingency, Irony, and Solidarity* (1989), Rorty believes ethical change hinges on listening to and understanding innovative ideas and voices, and rooting out wrongdoing may not be apparent when observing behavior. Indeed, literature for Rorty, "especially the novel," inspires empathy and challenges people to "com[e] to see other human beings as 'one of us' rather than as 'them'" (Rorty, 1989, p. XVI). Rorty believes literature is necessary to expose injustices and create understanding. Works of fiction examine humanity's unpredictability, but they also unpack discrete notions of truth and compassion. They unpack me.

References

Bakhtin, M. M. (1981). *The dialogic imagination: Four essays* (C. Emerson & M. Holquist, Trans.; M. Holquist, Ed.). University of Texas Press. (Original work published 1934–1935)

Bok, S. (1989). *Lying: Moral choice in public and private life*. Vintage Books.

Burke, K. (1969). *A grammar of motives*. University of California Press.

Berger, J., (Writer), Sontag, S. (Writer), & Lloyd, M. (Director). (1983, February 9). To tell a story (Season 1, Episode 7). [TV series episode]. In Eichler, U. (Producer), *Voices*. Channel 4 BBC, Brook Productions.

Holquist, M. (1981). Introduction (C. Emerson, and Holquist, M., Trans.). In M. Holquist (Ed.), *The dialogic imagination: Four essays* (pp. XV–XXXIV). University of Texas Press.

Kneupper, C. W. (1978). Teaching argument: An introduction to the Toulmin model. *College Composition and Communication*, 29(3), 237–241. https://doi.org/10.2307/356935

McGowan, C. (2024). *Cherry bomb* [Unpublished manuscript].

O'Brien, T. (1990). How to tell a true war story. In *The things they carried* (pp. 67–85). Broadway Books.

Rorty, R. (1989). *Contingency, irony, and solidarity* (1st ed.). Cambridge University Press.

Rorty, R. (2010). Redemption from egotism: James and Proust as spiritual exercises. In C. J. Voparil & R. J. Bernstein (Eds.), *The Rorty reader* (pp. 389–406). Wiley-Blackwell.

Swift, J. (2005). *Gulliver's travels into several remote regions of the world* (T. M. Balliet, Ed.) [E-book]. Project Gutenberg. (Original work published 1726)

Toulmin, S. E. (2003). *The uses of argument* (2nd ed.). Cambridge University Press.

CHAPTER 4

A Fight for Words

L'esprit de l'escalier

> I like the feeling of being able to confront an experience and resolve
> it as art.
>
> EUDORA WELTY, "*Paris Review, #55*"

∴

I work through trouble in stories—my own and the world's. My tales teem with conflict and the aftermath of pain. The perilous recent decades of my life, all at sixes and sevens, were full of pratfalls, puffery, and pranks. Sure, all lives have hurdles, but mine are impossible to jump. My most serious mistake to date was revealing a secret I had kept close. Yes, in 2016, I published an essay about an incident I had not discussed for decades.

I was raped when I was 18, and I finally wrote about it. It was a life-altering error. Why? After the piece appeared online for all the world to see, my revelations deeply shocked and surprised my colleagues at the college where I taught. Comments in passing or via email ranged from condemnation to doubt:

"You've never mentioned you were raped ... are you certain this is true?" [Yes, it is true.]

"This is fiction, right? Yeah, you're a fiction writer." [It was not fiction.]

"Are you this desperate for attention?" [Never.]

After months of being barraged with doubt, hostile comments, and passive-aggressive actions, I resigned.

Since that dark time, I have doubted my voice. I worry if literature has the potential for good or can elicit change. And I understood how any personal revelation might harm an author. But literature is essential to others, so I have soldiered on as a reader and writer, hoping to rehabilitate my optimism. Literature opens doors to empathy and understanding, providing a cathartic escape from life's hardships.

These days, I write with a different aim. Writing is how I handle accumulated pain, examining women's lives to reveal how society treats victims; I intend to be an older woman who speaks her truth. Just as I appreciate pieces pushing boundaries, I challenge limits. I aim and shoot high; often, I miss. Over the decades,

© CATE MCGOWAN, 2025 | DOI:10.1163/9789004712379_004

I have authored enough stories and poems following "accepted" approaches. I wrote those pieces to please others with whatever they imparted as "right." Whatever "right" is. Now, I write for myself and women who are like me. Right?

• • •

I read across different platforms to improve my writing skills. In my undergraduate years, a poetry mentor said, "Read a hundred poets; write like a hundred different poets. Read a thousand poets; write like yourself." My skepticism about writing rules helps me tackle projects with fresh eyes and ears. It is my way of defying the established norms. Another well-meaning writing teacher told our class how stories should never end with the main character dying or with the words, "And then I woke up." In my narrative "Poppies," a bear often visits the narrator in her dreams. I end the tale emphasizing my defiance towards conventions: "I know it's a cliché to end a story with, *and then I woke up,* but I did, and this is not an ending, anyway" (McGowan, 2020b, para. 26). Writers should not strive to break all writing rules, but must question them.

A writing rule most beginning authors learn to heed is the maxim about "Chekhov's gun." Over a century ago, fiction writer and playwright Anton Chekhov exhorted that each element in a story must serve a purpose (Gurlyand, 1904, p. 521). Paraphrasing Chekhov's well-known illustration, if a play introduces a handgun sitting on a table in the first act, by the last act, someone should fire the gun; otherwise, why include it onstage? Chekhov exhorted to ditch any unnecessary details in a narrative and focus instead only on elements that contribute to it, regardless of their apparent relevance at the outset.

While adhering to the concept of "Chekhov's gun" has become a staple rule of creative writing, I am drawn instead to the absurdity of randomly placing objects or people in stories. Life is random—and inserting strangeness for strangeness' sake makes no sense and does not further the plot. Yet, unexpected, out-of-left-field weirdness might hew closer to real life's unforeseen turns. Each day, unexplainable events happen, and often, there is no practical purpose for "happenings," as Tim O'Brien would call them. As Susan Sontag explains:

> At the very center of the whole enterprise of storytelling, there is the fact that storytelling is an activity that faces in two directions. On the one hand, it's connected with an idea of truth. On the other hand, it's connected with an idea of invention, imagination, lies. One is thrilled by the story precisely because it describes something that can't *happen* [emphasis added]. It's connected with fantasy. (Berger et al., 1983, 5:38–6:00)

The distinction between the explained and the random or fabulist event is at the heart of the differences between Modernism and Postmodernism. Yes, Chekhov's concern about unnecessary props was one of purpose, and if one follows the Russian dramatist's reasoning, each word and detail in a play, story, or poem should benefit the work's forward thrust. I concur. What if my narratives could be less straightforward? Sometimes, Chekhov's gun does not serve the story's meaning, and the writer should strike it. Shifting the logic, what if a weapon suddenly materialized on a desk during the last act? Imagine the plot suddenly turning and the characters needing a firearm once the play concludes.

And what of James Joyce's epiphany theory? The boy's intense disappointment strikes us hard when we read Joyce's "Araby" (1914/2018). What is the point? Does the reader need closure after the boy purchases nothing for his crush at the bazaar when he encounters not the magical place of his imagination, but the dingy reality? No, we instead feel sad when the boy has an epiphany about the pointlessness of it all: "Gazing up into the darkness I saw myself as a creature driven and derided by vanity; and my eyes burned with anguish and anger" (Joyce, 1914/1993, p. 22). Tying the story into a neat bow at its conclusion would not leave the boy feeling inconsequential after his first glimpse at how the adult world works.

Stories do not need resolutions. Reading a story validates a story, even those without closure. I appreciate tales attempting to convey the authenticity of feelings—even messy narratives that others might deride. All the knowledge I continue gaining and the language I have absorbed inform my work. The more I know, the more I accept various approaches to a problem. I would never impose my limited knowledge on anyone. I only know myself. As an editor, though, I may be a judging, trustworthy reader; as an author, I trust my readers to be the arbiters.

•••

I am tired of navigating the aftermath of my sexual assault. And it is challenging to cope in a society rejecting various gender roles. Discussions about sexual violence these days often elicit questions about what people mean when they label another person a "woman." Usually, these discussions focus on the tension between constructing a shared identity for women and abolishing gender categories altogether.

In *On Violence and On Violence Against Women* (2021), Jacqueline Rose wrestles with this problem and cautions against using the word "woman" uncritically. Rose uses the lenses of literature and psychoanalysis to process and explain violent acts against women. Her primary argument is that violence is part of gendered discourse:

> [V]iolence against women is a crime of the deepest thoughtlessness. It is a sign that the mind has brutally blocked itself. The best way for feminism to counter violence against women ... is to speak of, to stay and reckon with, the extraordinary, often painful and mostly overlooked range of what the human mind is capable of. (Rose, 2021, pp. 174–175)

As Rose notes, relying on a category of gender might make it easier to justify violence against women. Indeed, essays about male domination can be less convincing when they only rely on gendered categories. Rose also contends that writing might help create spaces where gendered violence can be identified and confronted—she turns to literature written by women throughout her studies to process the violence done to our bodies, the violent acts humans think about: "[L]iterature remains for me the place where, as part of the ever more urgent bid to change the world, the unthinkable can still be written and heard: 'unspeakable things unspoken,' in Toni Morrison's words" (Rose, 2021, p. 158). According to Rose, critical inquiries encourage looking at potential biases inherent in language.

To comprehend violence directed at women, critics must explore how male writers have formed narratives and portrayals of women and, even if their effects are unintentional, how they promote misogyny. By examining narrative representations, we can highlight how scapegoated females face punishment for their vulnerability in unjust systems, a society often blaming women for cultural problems created by men's violent campaigns. Gendered subjugation is a problem caused by society's physical and economic violence, its minimization of damage, the "quiet conditions, ... [and] the skill with which capital cloaks its crimes" (Rose, 2021, p. 6).

• • •

Every day, I doubt myself. I side-eye my mirror and long for the Scooby-Doo cartoon double-mask-reveal, wanting to pull off this unhappy older woman's disguise to expose a more pleasant façade, to stand from a chair with no stiffness. Tackle terrors. Float in quicksand. But I suspect I am instead a car crash pile-up, a lightning strike, dropping ACME anvils and boxes of dynamite to foil myself, but unlike animated characters, I do not recover from cliff falls or hitting brick walls; I do not survive rolling avalanches and ten-ton boulders squashing me. Life is a blunderbuss backfiring, a shitshow of furled parachutes, silverware shrapnel. Somebody has painted a fake tunnel on the side of a mountain going nowhere.

Yet.

I may yet conjure the words to set myself free. I must trust my voice; beginning with anger is an excellent place to commence.

In Ara Osterwiel's manifesto, "FUCK YOU! A Feminist Guide to Surviving the Art World," she states, "[W]e live in a world that's so totally fucked that sometimes the only possible response is to acknowledge it with a response of animosity. Even if it means having to use the F-word (by which I mean *feminist*)" (2016, p. 321).

Cussing calms me. Sometimes, the most satisfying speech is salty speech. Consider the old saying, "That man cusses like a sailor." Well, I am an elite Navy Seal on my fourth tour of duty. In my limited sphere, profanity is a sorting hat—a separator. Out, out, faint of heart! Indeed, coarse language helps me cull all the prissy folk who do not care to be in my presence as I fling profanities. Rough speech defines how I perceive an abstract physical world with jarring specificity and brevity—I do not have time to lollygag.

• • •

Welcome to the Deep South.

As soon as I could talk, I was a word magnet, a budding know-it-all who sponged up all I could learn and use to my advantage—including cussing. Funny, I never overheard my mother use less-than-proper language, and I only heard my father utter an off-color word once.

One evening, when I was five, I improved my vocabulary slant-wise. After a long day of thunderstorms, it was a swampy July twilight, the sun disappearing in slow degrees behind violet clouds. I sat on the front lawn under the shade of a low-limbed oak and spied on my father, who was tinkering in the car in the driveway. He leaned over our station wagon, Betsy, and wrestled with new windshield wipers, struggling to install them. Those obstinate blades would not stay put—each time my father attempted to secure a wiper to an arm, the rubber lash flipped back at him, slapping his chest from the released tension. Dad switched sides, sliding the black rubber sheath along the other metal-armed lever. He stretched out the wiper and tamped it down; it sprung loose. Dad switched to the other side. No luck. After many minutes of attempts, Dad's fingers were bloody from his fruitless efforts, and he was furious.

"Damn you, Betsy! DAMN you, damn you, DAMN, DAMN, DAMN!"

I had never heard the word and yelled from where I crouched in the summer grass, "Hey, Dad! What's 'damn' mean?" He did not know I was listening.

He shielded his eyes against the twilight sun as he turned to face me. "Well, it means pretty much the same as *darn*."

"Oh, okay." I filed it away. It was an exciting word, packing more punch than its watered-down cousin, "Darn."

I used my unfamiliar word a few weeks later when someone enlisted me to play badminton with other kids and parents at the Sacred Heart Church picnic. I gave the game my best, but I was just a kid playing with older kids, and the net was so high. Each time I missed a volley or scrubbed returning the shuttlecock, I yelled my fury.

"DAMN! Damn, damn, damn, damn." I made it into a song.

Though I never saw Mom spectating, I now can picture her sitting in a lounge chair, taking in the badminton game with the other church ladies. Then I screamed, "DAMN!" for the last time. Mom yanked me by my collar off the lawn, and we left the rest of the family at the picnic.

Mom dragged me down the hall to the bathroom at home, pointed at the closed toilet, and said, "You sit down there where you belong, Miss Potty Mouth!" She grabbed a bar of Life Buoy soap and lathered up my toothbrush. "Open your mouth!"

I dropped my jaw, and she scrubbed out my mouth, scouring with the enthusiasm of a true believer. She did not stop as I gagged and choked at the sharp taste.

"You WILL NEVER use that word again. Ever." But I was unsure what the scrubbing had to do with the word "damn," and I did not understand how soap would banish the words I preferred.

I did not learn. I endured sudsy punishments for years to come for all kinds of infractions, and my palate deadened to the nasty taste of Life Buoy or Irish Spring or whatever brand my mother found on sale. One time, I called my best friend's brother "Clark the fart." I had no idea what a fart was, but I appreciated the phrase's slant rhyme, those lovely, growling Rs, and how the words made Clark, a smart aleck, cry.

• • •

I was a plucky kid, and I still project gutsiness in casual circumstances, but deep down, life has made me more fragile than I appear. Out of earshot, I will whisper, "Fuck you," but I seldom say it loud enough. Age has softened my edges, but when I was young, I suspected words were a ticket out of my bleak family milieu. I made sharp observations, offending many, especially my mother. I could write, and I resolved never to have kids or be a stay-at-home parent, nurse, secretary, or any other role my grandfather once informed me were the only proper pursuits for females. But the world happened to me, and I discovered shame is a powerful muzzle. Nowadays, I am a cautious adult—I read a room before I speak.

In my younger years, I flirted with danger. But like all those occasions when I continued using profanity as a kid, I did not learn. In my late teens, I pushed boundaries, placing myself in harm's way to prove a point. One time, I remember tempting fate when I stepped on a banana peel as an experiment— that over-used slapstick gag in TV sitcoms was not real! So, I trod on a smashed plantain in a parking lot and skated across the blacktop. *Splat!* After my skid- out, I lay there, wearing a halo of circling birdies. My broken tailbone took months to heal.

• • •

I was raped when I was eighteen.

• • •

When I was eighteen, I learned a lesson. Being sexually assaulted was not the lesson.

No, I discovered that most people, even those I love, cannot be trusted.

• • •

One night, after a fun time of clubbing, a stranger raped me and left me half- clothed in my Honda. I had walked with my friends into the dark lot where we had all parked, air-kissed everyone goodbye, and watched them back out onto Peachtree Road. They left. I stood alone under a streetlight, fumbling for my car keys. As I opened my door, someone pushed me from behind, and I was soon face down in the backseat. A man kneeled on top of me and held a gun to my temple. With one hand, he pulled down my skirt, rolled me to face him, and demanded I undo his pants. He climbed on top of me.

Yes, it was terrifying and demeaning and nightmarish; I will not minimize what happened, but the violation's aftermath was so much worse than the violation. After the man left me in my car and ran down the desolate side- walk, yelling his last threats over his shoulder, I hobbled to a payphone to call a friend. She called the police and then came to pick me up.

At the emergency room doors, a female police officer and nurse were wait- ing for me. Their hours-long joint examination was grueling and demeaning; they took photographs and hair samples and fluid swabs. After many questions and physical probes, the stern examination nurse wheeled me through the hospital to an in-patient room. I never saw her smile. She placed a business card on the side table as I sat on the bed.

"It's a contact number for Dr. Jones. You should call him. And, um, we've notified your family. I know you told us not to, but we did," she said and slammed the door as she left.

A few days later, my mother and sister appeared at my bedside. They had been to Sunday Mass and were wearing their church clothes—starched linen and shiny heels—and my mother spoke in her bless-your-heart voice.

"What happened?" Translation: *How could my daughter have done this to me?*

"Well, I can't believe you came to *Grady*." Translation: *Grady Hospital isn't for upstanding people like us.*

"Only tramps go out and get themselves raped." Translation: *I taught you better.* Translation: *And you're a slut.* Translation: *And it's your fault.*

My mother did not need to wash my mouth with soap this time—shame was much more effective.

I responded, "Fuck you."

My mother and sister walked out.

•••

In *On Violence*, Rose discusses how she believes women enacting personal agency in our society is impossible. Rose also argues that we must resist the expressions of influence targeting women. Historically, cultures have often idealized women as images of "masculinity in a panic" or a projection of masculine identity itself, especially in times of struggle or political conflict (Rose, 2021, p. 48), also described as "impotent bigness," a term Rose borrows from Hannah Arendt (p. 6). This state of "impotent bigness" might also enable the exploration of self-confidence as an attribute often associated with masculinity. Still, it is an idealized distortion designating perceived threats—sometimes acting on them.

Psychoanalysis illuminates how two values shape gender roles, "allotted sexual roles" (Rose, 2021, p. 365), which indicates equating masculinity with violence is too binary an instinct: "[E]ven while calling out masculinity in its worst guise, we allow to individual men the potential gap between maleness and the infinite complexity of the human mind" (p. 9). Women do not receive the same courtesy.

In short, blaming all violence on men is also a cop-out, but society gives them a pass for their actions and regards them as discrete individuals who are acting on human, not male, instincts when they lash out. Rose wants us to work for novel frameworks to understand the role of violence committed by and on others. She wants us to confront and reflect on the various forms of structural violence, allowing the perpetuation of harm to portions of the population.

Nonetheless, we live in an era when women are held accountable for men's sins, when females are expected to "clean up the world" and make it tolerable so men do not have to experience any darkness women witness (Rose, 2021, p. 365). And if men do not experience the direct harms perpetrated on women, they are at least spared the pain too many women live through, the issues they will never encounter.

Society designates the roles of masculine and feminine, but we should not have to adhere to such essentialism. Our society has a choice. Our initial reaction, a human's first instinct, is often to blame ourselves or others rather than examine our actions. When violence occurs, people frequently blame victims or focus on punishing the culprit rather than implementing solutions. We must ask why a terrible event happened and fix the cause. We must resist accusations and focus on answers. We must enact solidarity in the healing process, recognizing that collective power can belong to us all.

If others heal, I might. If I can heal, I know others might.

• • •

I did what I was supposed to do—I contacted the police, visited the hospital, and endured a grueling interrogation. Not once, but twice. I was prodded, plucked, and photographed at the hospital. Later, the police dusted my car for fingerprints.

When the Atlanta Police Department (APD) called me into their headquarters two weeks after I was attacked, I was sure they were hot on the trail of my assailant. That day, when I entered the APD's building, the officers spirited me into a cramped, windowless room and grilled me. They implied the rape was my fault. All the detectives were male; each got their turn with me, asking for personal details while showing no interest when I tried to answer. And though, weeks later, the blue bruises on my arms and face remained visible, despite the photographic evidence of my assault in my case folder, despite their forensic samples of my attacker's skin from under my fingernails, his semen and hair swabbed and combed from my battered face, genitals, and thighs, they did not believe me. They did not believe me. They did not believe me. They did not believe it.

• • •

I have come to terms with how I feel about that awful night when a stranger attacked me. I have also learned that people are often not kind. Most importantly, though, I focus on genuine expressions of myself. By changing how I see the world, I find a place where I am appreciated. And I refuse to be silenced, especially in my storytelling. It is how I have healed.

Of course, I now know, after being "violated" so soon after the attack by that rape kit examination in the hospital and the cynical detectives who had my case, that the cops never worked to apprehend my perpetrator.

They never tested my confiscated underwear or skin.

No forensic specialist tested the semen and skin and hair samples; no desk jockey compared the stranger's fingerprints from my car to those on record; no officer made inquiries at the nightclub or asked my friends questions.

The authorities did nothing. And I waited. For years, nightmares plagued me, and I imagined the daunting task before me—I would someday have to identify my rapist. I avoided entire swaths of Atlanta's metropolitan area for fear of being attacked or seeing my attacker. I developed an impenetrable shell.

Though I dreaded it for years, I wished the APD would call me with an investigation update. But the phone never rang.

In the fall of 2019, I read the Pulitzer Prize-winning essay "An Unbelievable Story of Rape" by T. Christian Miller and Ken Armstrong (2015). The article explained a circumstance like my own—it was eerie. And I realized how traumatizing it is for a survivor of sexual assault when no one cares or believes them. Thousands of others can relate. For decades, many hundreds of thousands of other American sexual assault survivors have faced institutional dismissal. I was like Marie, the 2015 essay's subject; no one with any power cared or gave my story credence.

After my chance encounter with Miller and Armstrong's article, I discovered ongoing efforts by victim advocacy groups to uncover untested forensic medical exams (FMEs), also known as rape kits, the evidence collected after a sexual assault. I found another article in *the Atlanta Journal and Constitution (AJC)* detailing an investigation into Georgia's backlogged FMEs (Mariano, 2015a). Mariano, the reporter for the *AJC*, also discovered over 1,500 rape kits collecting dust in the basement of Grady (2015b), the hospital I visited after I was raped. Grady had never released the kits to investigators at the APD or the Georgia Bureau of Investigation (GBI). I realized no one had even looked for my attacker, and I am sure the hospital staff and police ignored the FME containing the DNA evidence needed to identify my attacker.

In Mariano's article, I found a helpful link to an online contact form at the Georgia Victim Notification Portal, which I filled out, and a week later, administrators from the Georgia Sexual Assault Kit Initiative Task Force and the

Criminal Justice Coordinating Council telephoned me. In those long conversations, the women reassured me that law enforcement approaches to assault had changed in the years since my attack. And we cried together. They assured me they would search for my FME and find the police report containing the details of my assault. I also found out that the latest news reports had only revealed untested rape kits dating back to 2000; they suspected Grady had hundreds more forgotten FMEs tracing back to the early 1980s.

Unfortunately, and not surprisingly, the task force found no police report about my assault, so they could not search for the FME. With no police report, they hit a dead end. No one could mount an investigation. My experience is not unusual: In America, over 400,000 kits in the United States, some decades old, remain untested (Joyful Heart Foundation, n.d.). Perhaps the police did not lose my information; they destroyed it or did not file it. My rape kit is probably still in Grady's basement.

• • •

When we seek to belong, we women often place ourselves in precarious positions by communing with the very same people who might oppress us. The tension of this irony exists in several of my stories. Society cages my characters, not allowing them true freedom; they are psychic prey. In her 2022 *New Yorker* review of Cristina Rivera Garza's body of work, Merve Emre explains how writers must reveal the physical harms perpetrated on women. She explains author Rivera Garza's approach to violence against women:

> It is the state that is responsible for the mutilated bodies that lie by the roadside, even if its smiling politicians and bland technocrats do not wield the blades themselves. And the responsibility of the writer? Confronted with these bodies, she must express, "In the most basic and also the most disjointed language possible, *This hurts me*." (Emre, 2022, p. 79)

Sure, my language can be "basic" and "disjointed," but at least now I can tell people what happened to me.

For years, I had no way of articulating how damaged I was. As someone unseen and not believed, I never uttered the extent of my pain. I put on a brave face. I was cheerful and easygoing. At least, that was what I wanted people to think. Now, I believe my job as an author is to expose who and what has hurt me.

It is essential to inform people about the harm perpetrated by hegemonic systems and, in my case, to let people know about anyone who refuses to help women. I must scratch at the veneer of patriarchal mechanisms seeking to control women. Most importantly, I must show how we deal with a society working to exclude women at all costs.

• • •

I stopped speaking in contractions seven years ago when I left my teaching position, when I quit under duress. And in my creative work, my diction has altered to more formal expressions. When I drafted this book, I vacillated between using more informal contractions or writing out the words. I chose to write out the words and avoided truncating them. What has changed? I attribute this communication-style shift to the trauma of a recent disclosure about my sexual assault.

When I shared my essay recounting a stranger's assault on me, I was once again at the mercy of not being believed. I had to fight against that doubt all over again, and in doing so, I lost my career and friends who labeled me a liar. As a result, changing my language style was not just about dropping contractions; it also meant losing faith in others and myself.

But the written word strengthens me; writing is my way of rising above. I use it like a weapon, refusing to sugarcoat or hold back for fear of jeopardizing my livelihood. However, I try to refrain from cruel utterances or shouting "FUCK YOU" from the rooftops. Finding the right words to convey my feelings is challenging—especially in the heat of the moment. Often, I only think of clever comebacks after I walk away from an argument; French call it *l'esprit d'escalier* (staircase wit).

Unlike confronting someone face-to-face, shouting my feelings in writing is always acceptable; I can say whatever I want. When crafting a poem or story, I do not experience *l'esprit d'escalier* when I think of a retort. I get it down and out. But I often need to remind myself to stay true to what I want to say instead of getting caught up in mellifluous verbiage. Sometimes, that means letting go of phrases or sentences I love that do not serve a composition in progress. To borrow from Faulkner, I kill my darlings.

My life's work is saying what I mean and providing a way of looking at the world that a reader might not have considered before. I prefer to employ whatever words are most effective, whether they echo the sounds of my Southern upbringing or engage in academic rhetoric. I use words to help people or further an idea's meaning, aiming not to harm anyone. In his famous shtick "The Seven Words You Can't Say on Television," Comedian George Carlin referred to the obscene language as words "we won't use all the time, just sometimes" (1972, 41:52). So, let us open the language floodgates. Dive in—the water is fucking fine.

Healing means not letting other people define who I am. It means trying to understand that the oppression of women permeates our society. We must act for change. Sticks and stones? Bruises? Heck, injuries heal. Washing my mouth out with soap? I can learn to love the flavor of Life Buoy. Silence me? Never again.

I speak up more. I channel my fearless child self, a brave girl from long ago who chose punishment over silence and the taste of soap suds over staying quiet. These extraordinary times call for resistance to defend what is right. Ara Osterweil proposes refusing to take aggressions sitting down—her endorsement of provocative profanity for protest suits me: "FUCK YOU is not only an act of self-exposure but a philosophical provocation to consider the meaning of a blazing signifier" (2016, p. 322). Blazing is the way to fight. These days, as duplicitous public figures spout "alternative facts," promoting corruption, espionage, and human rights violations, we must resist their efforts. And though ad hominem attacks are not my bread and butter, defending others (and myself) might entail what I call cathartic cussing. These days, when I am angry, I am not above using choice words.

I will say FUCK YOU when I need to say it. I will fight for my words and my being. As Osterwiel proclaims, "FUCK YOU is a way of saying that even when you do everything you can to fuck my body, you can never fuck ME" (2016, p. 322).

References

Armstrong, K., & Miller, T. C. (2016). An unbelievable story of rape. In S. Holt (Ed.), *The best American Magazine writing 2016* (pp. 203–242). Columbia University Press.

Carlin, G. (1972). Seven words you can never say on television. On *Class Clown* [MP3]. Atlantic.

Berger, J. (Writer), Sontag, S. (Writer), & Lloyd, M. (Director). (1983, February 9). To tell a story (Season 7, Episode 1) [TV series episode]. In U. Eichler (Producer), *Voices*. Channel 4 BBC, Brook Productions.

Emre, M. (2022, July 11 & 18). Bodies politic. *The New Yorker*, 76–79.

Gurlyand, I. (1904, July 11). Reminiscences of A. P. Chekhov. *Teatr i iskusstvo, 28*.

Joyce, J. (1993). Araby. In *Dubliners*. Wordsworth. (Original work published 1914)

Joyful Heart Foundation. (n.d.). End the rapekit backlog. Retrieved March 23, 2024, from https://www.endthebacklog.org/

Mariano, W. (2015a, July 30). Grady releasing 1000 rape kits withheld from law enforcement. *Atlanta Journal-Constitution*. https://www.ajc.com/news/state--regional-govt--politics/grady-releasing-000-rape-kits-withheld-from-law-enforcement/lmNadPDErZa3CNBQmiEEoH/

Mariano, W. (2015b, August 2). Locked away. *Atlanta Journal-Constitution*.
    https://investigations.ajc.com/gradyrapekits/

McGowan, C. (2020). Poppies. *Riggwelter*(28). Retrieved March 23, 2024, from
    https://issuu.com/riggwelter/docs/issue_28

Miller, T. C., & Armstrong, K. (2015). *An unbelievable story of rape*. ProPublica.

Osterwiel, A. (2016, June 1). FUCK YOU! A feminist guide to surviving the art world.
    Artforum International. https://www.artforum.com/print/201606/a-feminist-guide-
    to-surviving-the-art-world-ara-osterweil-60103

Rose, J. (2021). *On violence and on violence against women*. Farrar, Straus and Giroux.

CHAPTER 5

Descanso

I have never been comfortable expressing emotions or writing about my life. Fiction is safe. A while ago, a writer friend mentioned she had composed a thousand-page memoir. I told her that detailed personal writing only leads to heartache—no one needs to know every detail about someone's life. I still believe memoirs should only be written by 80-year-old Nobel Laureates or 14-year-old Olympians who use ghostwriters. My friend has not spoken to me since our talk.

Not all memoirs are nonsense, but poetry and fiction are safer venues for *me*. In either genre, I can display my emotions in a cosplay cloak of someone else's joy and pain. Our current culture encourages over-sharing and demands personal stakes. Rita Felski notes in *Doing Time* (2000):

> It is a striking fact of scholarly life that talking about oneself has become a virtue. The culture of confession, once limited to self-help manuals, therapy groups, and talk shows, has gradually penetrated the academy's walls. For critics who are disenchanted with the spread of theory or want to explore different kinds of scholarly writing, autobiography can be an appealing alternative. Getting personal can take various forms, from a terse vignette prefacing a conventional piece of academic writing to a full-blown striptease by a scholar-superstar. Often, it is accompanied by an ethical imperative. I'm doing this, the author implies, and you should do it, too. (p. 33)

As Felski argues, public self-reflection is also symptomatic of celebrity culture and a society exalting individuality above privacy and civility.

But my reticence to share autobiographical details is also a by-product of my class and gender, which Felski confronts. However, she recognizes that "feminists, in particular, have often been at the vanguard of personal criticism, arguing that traditional forms of academic language need to be replaced by a more personal voice" (Felski, 2000, pp. 33–34). Personal essays, memoirs, and autobiographies can transgress in ways traditional scholarship cannot. Thus, I am attempting to master the scholarly personal narrative.

• • •

© CATE MCGOWAN, 2025 | DOI:10.1163/9789004712379_005

My father was not a lucky man, and I have worried about his misfortunes my entire adult life.[1] He died young and unaccomplished, but loved by many. I have written poetry about his passing and subsequent absence, trying to compensate for the lack of a father with many failed father-figure relationships; I have overachieved in my academic and work life, neglecting my relationships and health. Dad's passing shaped me more than my Catholic upbringing or my disappointment at not being the daughter my mom wanted. I am a neurotic, guilt-ridden woman who stays up late to check my grammar on social media. I keep most people at bay because I know they will leave me. And the people I let into my heart break it.

Often, I pass *descansos* and roadside memorials, and my gaze lingers on the flower bouquets, decorated crosses, dingy, weather-worn stuffed animals, and sometimes-lit seven-day candles propped in the grass. *Memento mori* curated on medians and curbs are places of active mourning. I yearn to create a *descanso* for my father. His gravesite, on a hillside with a dogwood shading the plot, is not a suitable testament that the man once existed. A gravestone is a cold, hard thing. When I visit his landscaped cemetery, a place with all the dead neatly lined up, I am walking through a glorified file cabinet. Graveyards are the dead's territory, not mine.

In the land of the living, *descansos* appear as improvised, fleeting markers. On a roadway, one can drive around a bend to find a *descanso* in the grassy median at a busy intersection with lit seven-day candles, muddy stuffed animals, and silk flower arrangements left to weather the elements. Someone has perished in this spot. Many of the items planted in monument piles are only meaningful to those who have died or put them there to memorialize their relative or friend—the teddy bear with a tennis racquet is a signifier devoid of meaning for anyone other than the bereaved.

The random presence of these makeshift monuments is often disturbing. There are two right now around the corner from where I live, planted on a dangerous curve where people continue to meet their ends. If only I could make a memorial for my father in the exact spot where he died; if only I could place a poesy for him there. Or a rosary. I would also leave a note for the others who died that day. But where did my father die? I would travel there to mark the place, but I must figure out how to find it.

• • •

In his opening remarks to *The Oxford Handbook of the Self* (2011), editor Shaun Gallagher offers an alternate view of our self-obsessed culture, articulating, "[O]ne of the most important developments in self-studies has been the realization that the self is a process, not a given, a constant work in progress, not a finished product" (p. 7). Rather than positioning intimate facts and details about the self (such as those in modern autobiographies), Gallagher attempts to hide the self behind a screen of conceptual theory. He writes, "What I have done is to write a series of vignettes in the first-person plural to articulate the contemporary sense of self as a collection of perspectives on a shifting series of objects" (Gallagher, 2011, p. 7). Rather than asking us to put ourselves on display as individuals, Gallagher asks us to acknowledge the importance of the other. We are not alone in our pursuits, scholarly or otherwise.

•••

My father's accident report from the Alabama State Troopers is long gone. My mother squirreled it away. It revealed concrete information about my father's fate, which is now lost. I do not remember all the details about how my father died, and I have no one left whom I can ask about it. Searching public records has proved a fruitless endeavor—I cannot locate information or news about the incident. However, for years, I have scoured rural Alabama newspaper microfiches and databases for articles about 1975 car crashes with multiple fatalities.

When I was an adolescent (13? or 15?), I remember reading the report my mother had hidden inside the living room secretary. Some Alabama state trooper scrawled the facts in barely legible handwriting, a blasé-sounding narrative: three dead, treacherous weather, a semi-truck. Dry, unemotional. It is a police report, not a sympathy card. And I am sure the wobbly handwriting belonged to the same dispassionate officer who called my mother the night my dad died.

Clipped to the multi-page document was a photograph. I can visualize it clearly if I close my eyes. In the black-and-white image, my father's behemoth Chevy is a pinched-up, wobbly triangle the size of a small house, an unrecognizable chunk of metal as if it had rolled down the face of a rock mountain. In the picture, a man in uniform stands beside the car and wears one of those wide-brimmed hats with a leather chin strap. Someone has placed pylons at equidistant intervals on the wet highway behind. The driver's door is at least six feet off the ground—the officer's hat only reaches the car's running board. And the door hangs slightly open, exposing the front seat, which is ripped and stained.

There is no way to survive a crash like that.

•••

I intend to share my personal journey, experiences, and ideas in this contextualization. We are all shaped by our life histories and experiences. These stories show how my life influenced my writing, how human lives are inextricably bound. I have no desire to limit my work to a series of anecdotes, avoiding the obvious pitfall of a series of "I" statements where I rationalize the formation of my subject position. A subject's position in scholarly discourse is tricky, and it is challenging to represent my ideas effectively with anecdotes. Conversely, the vignettes in this contextualization tell stories. How ironic.

I can recount the Alabama state trooper's phone call verbatim. My mother memorized it, too, repeating it to us so often that we knew it by heart.

"Ma'am, are you the wife of a Mr. McGowan, who resides at 1515 Inwood Road in Atlanta? Yes, well, he had a car accident today. He didn't survive ... No, lady, I'm not kidding. Lady, I don't make jokes like that." My mother often told us about that conversation with the trooper, her face reddening. Each time she recounted the conversation, she reopened our wounds. We could bond over the family's outrage about a stranger's insensitivity. How could someone be so cruel to a recent widow and mother of now-fatherless children? We hated that man throughout my childhood. My mother's face screwed tight whenever she relived picking up the phone that fateful evening. After receiving the news, I do not think she developed past the anger stage of grief.

These days, I imagine what it would take to make that call. It is the storyteller in me. I understand other perspectives, regardless of how painful, and I am sure it must have been agonizing to deliver the news of my father's accident. Who were we to fault him for sounding cold or think he was evil? I often engage in this empathy exercise—I have considered this man's story all my life and how his supposedly flippant delivery of such tragic news may have been not so glib. Of course, my mother could only tune in to the terrible news he delivered, and moments of shock do not promote empathy. She felt nothing but loss and pain. My fiction germinates from this deep place of understanding various perspectives.

Although the personal essay has been a viable form for academics since the sixteenth century, these days, it often resembles the form of a memoir. However, I have no intention of telling my life story; I want to position my experiences and writing within the context of society and scholarship to show how the world influences me. If I cannot locate the site where my dad perished, I can at least imagine what happened. Southern clichés that describe the smell of honeysuckle on a summer afternoon or peaceful cicada songs along a dusty two-lane highway are pointless. These images lack originality and cannot immerse me in the scene.

Instead, I imagine a storm whipping rain at dusk with terrible visibility over a rise. I place myself in my father's seat, a rosary wrapped around his fingers as he grips the wheel. And I attempt to understand the trooper on the other end of that long-ago call when he broke the horrible news to my mother and broke her heart.

Maybe he had my father's wallet in his hand. Perhaps he was examining one of our family snapshots Dad had tucked into his billfold. It is a heartbreaking scenario all around. But I have come to accept that I may never physically go to where my father died, but I can at least depict the feelings of loss and groundlessness I still experience, giving my fictional characters similar heavy loads to carry.

There is no grand narrative about my life, family, or writing. My stories fracture and go in strange directions. Maybe my brain broke along the way. But I can dredge the inescapable aspects of my life. A writer can isolate, magnify, and make parts of a specimen stand for the whole, and I attempt to amplify my authentic emotions in my short stories. If I relay the same stories repeatedly, I can figuratively hit the reader over the head as I drive home the point: "Here! This passage is what I feel about people and the state of the world."

Note

1 This essay adapts portions of my essay, "I'll Go Now," which appears in *Descansos: Words from the Wayside*, Darkhouse Books (McGowan, 2017).

References

Felski, R. (2000). *Doing time.* New York University Press.

Gallagher, S. (Ed.). (2011). *The Oxford handbook of the self* (1st ed.). Oxford University Press.

McGowan, C. (2015). Water has its own memory. *Peace and Justice Initiative Bi-Annual Newsletter, 6*(1), 7–8.

McGowan, C. (2017). I'll go now. In S. Carlson (Ed.), *Descansos: Words from the wayside* (pp. 5–12). Darkhouse Books.

CHAPTER 6

My Mother's Voice

I am an orphan. My father died when I was nine, and my mother suffered like Jesus Christ.

Fifteen years ago, Mom succumbed. It was from a broken heart.

We had a complicated relationship. Fraught. Despite our relationship's thorniness, Mom speaks to me as I go about my days. Advice. Admonitions. Answers to prayers offered to the universe. Yet she tortured me as much as I tortured her. It has taken me half my life to understand that her flaws were normal and human; her foibles were not cudgels explicitly wielded at me. Mom was coping as best she could in a society hostile to her role as a single female parent. Yes, she was coping. As I was growing up, I did not recognize all her kindness and the extra efforts she made to raise and educate me. Now, I know how difficult it must have been to rear a child who was hell-bent on self-destruction, especially with her frail heart, which I inherited.

•••

As an essential feminist/womanist strategy, the Motherline is an idea developed by feminist psychoanalyst Naomi Lowinsky in her book *Motherline* (1992): "The Motherline is a name ... for the oneness of body and psyche, for the experience of continuity among women" (pp. 20–21). Motherlines are a means to connect with what has come and what is yet to come among female relatives and peers: "Whenever women gather in circles or pairs, ... they tell one another stories from the Motherline. These are stories of female experience, psychological, and historical ... of the life cycles that link ... women" (Lowinsky, 1992, p. 17).

Searching for the Motherline includes a woman's "journey back to her female roots" by engaging with ancestors and understanding the past, our birth and the births of children, and the lands from which they hail (Lowinsky, 1992, p. 29). Lowinsky claims women's souls have a tie to their mothers: "We, as a nation, are immigrants. Our people come from faraway lands, usually from terrible circumstances: famine, war, political and religious persecution. ... Our feminine souls are rooted in the Motherline" (1992, pp. 232–233).

The concept of Motherlines can promote women's issues, synthesizing disparate elements of females' experience and acting as resistance to Western white patriarchal narratives, their fragmentation, and their uses.

• • •

Female voices, not priests' admonitions, are the ones I turn to whenever I need reassurance, encouragement, or a kick in the pants. I have required a feminine voice to help me through the previous few years. I understand I am on the downslope of life—I have fewer years ahead than years spent. The womanly voice I have needed is my own. If it is a voice in the wilderness I have ignored, I understand it may be my spirit crying out for me. I have neglected my *nous*, "the angel of the soul," Mary Magdalene spoke about in her eponymous Gospel (Leloup, 2002, p. 13).

For me, an agnostic-sometimes-atheist pragmatist, non-tangible considerations are blasphemy, turning my back on all my hard-headed philosophical excuses for neglecting an inner light. Recently, I traced my way to Saint Teresa of Ávila's architecture of mansions, her explanation of pathways leading to a person's center, their "interior castle" (1588/2008). We might reside in peace if we focus on goodness and love. I can walk the path.

With female mystics, I have learned that words possess vibratory power. As I continue to study their works, the female mystics provide acceptance, a different kind than I ever needed from my mother. I lost my center in seeking what I could never accomplish with her. In the process of losing connectedness, I also lost my mother. Her voice grows dimmer these days unless I focus on my memories. I am acquainting myself with these new spiritual ideas to rediscover my true self and maintain my mother's voice speaking to me through each moment of my life.

• • •

At my mother's funeral in an old downtown Atlanta church on a late March morning, I sat in the front pew with my siblings; my husband held my hand. My mother's casket sat on metal risers at the front, below the altar.

The family priest at the pulpit chose my mother's funeral as the time to bring me back into the fold. I am a recovering Roman Catholic who will never return to the Church. I am my family's shame. Father Hernandez gave the requisite homily about my mother's deep faith and how she had received many of her sacraments under those same gold vaulted ceilings.

"I picture the woman we're mourning as a little girl in each scene—her Confession was in the back in one of those stalls." He gestured to the rear of the sanctuary, and everyone looked. "Her First Communion and Confirmation were up here." The crowd turned forward in their pews and stared at the altar, and Father Hernandez locked eyes with me, preaching the rest of his officious sermon. "Faith's an investment: You must give to it what you wish to receive. Like saving your fork when you go for a second round at a buffet, faith's holding onto what's essential or turning away from the Church."

I have never saved my fork and counted on the future. It is folly to expect safety, yet I am growing to trust my voice and the words of the oppressed. The here and now is essential to me; actions speak louder than intentions.

• • •

My mother emphasized dates because they marked milestones in her life, and she was a festive person. She was never one to miss a holy day of obligation in the Catholic Church. If the paper calendar she had taped on the refrigerator listed a holy day, Mom high-tailed it to Mass, and she would celebrate and sing in her off-tune way.

My birthday was a holy day for her, too. We had the same routine on my birthday when my mother was alive. She would tell me the story of my birth. Perhaps it was epic to her; my mother's recounting would convey as saccharine-sweet or mundane to most people. But she loved me. She would wake me early in her annoyingly cheerful way, scuffle into my bedroom, and then recount the same tale in the same cadence she had each year of my life, reciting a memorized litany. Her drawl was ragged in the early morning, and the story stayed the same. *Let me tell you about the day you were born.* After I moved away from home, Mom continued telling my story on morning birthday calls. My birthday narrative was my mother's storytelling, my mother's "Motherlining"—the importance of my coming into existence, the core of her existence. Now that she has been gone for years, I am lonely and anchorless without her, especially on my birthdays when I reach for a ringing phone, expecting Mom on the other end.

• • •

When I was young, Mom and I would forage in our suburb, strolling through front yards to pick crabapples and ripe figs in neighbors' trees (with permission, of course). We braved blackberry briars in abandoned, kudzu-covered fields alongside state two-lane highways. Some early summer mornings, we would hustle to the state farmers' market, where she taught me how to haggle for a reasonable price. The sun-shriveled men who sat on their tailgates, truck beds piled high with fresh produce, never saw my mother coming—she would talk them down on any price, and we would head home with a haul.

At home, we would boil jars in a pot on the stove to sterilize the containers for canning. We would lug our plunder inside, all the okra, squash, onions, peppers, and fruits we collected. After we sorted, I tugged on my mother's smallest apron, and she would place a metal step stool at the sink. I climbed up, brushed and washed each item over the basin. Next, it was chopping time. I moved my stool to the counter, and Mom would hand me a paring knife the perfect size for my child's hand, and I sliced each vegetable or fruit into neat quarter pieces or half-rounds until I emptied an entire crate or basket.

After we processed the produce, it was time to stew it on a low flame. We stirred veggies on a backburner and cooked fruits such as peaches and strawberries on low flames in front because sugary foods were more apt to scorch. From our sweltering kitchen, the scent of cloves and peppers and caramelized sugar wafted for hours through the house, and though we staggered whirring box fans down the hallway and our attic ventilator roared, the draft was no match for the gas stove's burners on those summer mornings.

As the jars cooled on the windowsill, my mother told me we had performed the same labor she and her mother had done, what her mother's mother had done, and what all the women in our family had done for generations. We were doing the essential work of providing for members of our family.

When I canned and pickled with my mother, I created a product from raw ingredients, contributing to my family's nourishment. As an adult, each time I sit down to write, I experience meaning, as I did when I worked with my mother. Authorship may not be as essential as canning and storing vegetables for winter, but drafting stories is necessary for me.

• • •

After I was nine, my darkest days were spring days after Dad died. The summer activities I once enjoyed, those mornings spent helping my mother and afternoons swimming at the pool, were gone. I begged off birthday parties and sleepaway camp. I stuck close to home and played catch with laconic boys who avoided chitchat. And I became moody. I retreated to a world I shared with no one. I played on creek banks, scouted songbirds, and created imaginary kingdoms of leaves, rocks, and mud. I designed imaginary castle interiors in my bedroom filled with what I thought were antiques and the dolls I collected. And books, I lived in books.

• • •

One of my mother's criticisms haunts me. After reading my first published story, she asked, "Why are you writing such depressing stuff? Who wants to read this? You need to write stories like the ones in *Woman's Day* magazine." A few months later, I relayed this exchange to the author, Dorothy Allison, during an interview for the newspaper where I worked. She laughed and replied, "Sweetie, that's what mamas say." My mother's attempts to censor my material were less novel than I thought. I was not the suffering artist I imagined myself to be.

In *Letters Home by Sylvia Plath: Correspondence 1950–1963*, Plath angrily declares to her mother, Aurelia, "Don't talk to me about the world needing cheerful stuff!" (1975, p. 473). In another correspondence, Plath demands her mother "stop trying to get me to write about 'decent, courageous people'—read the *Ladies' Home Journal* for those" (1975, p. 477). Of course, Plath was battling her own demons as a new mother, and she did not win. Society does not care about mothers' mental health. No one cared about my mother's feelings or plight. That is why I chose not to bear any children.

• • •

These essays are not a creation story, but a tale of dismantling complexity. My mother was a woman full of contradictions. The contradictions have seeded much of my torment. While I recuperated in the hospital after being sexually assaulted, she did not comfort me. She made me ashamed. But also, weeks later, I discovered no one during my rape kit examination had given me the morning-after pill—I was pregnant with my attacker's spawn. When I revealed my condition to my mother, she went against the tenets of Catholicism and drove me to an abortion clinic. She waited in the lobby for my procedure, and when I emerged from the operation groggy and crying, she took me home and tucked me in. The irony is that day was the closest she ever got to having a grandchild. And it is the closest I ever got to giving her another generation. I regularly worry about how she gave me life, and I did not return the favor.

Months after we visited the clinic, Mom told me she had gone to Penance the following Saturday. In the confessional box, she informed the priest he would never tell her what it was to protect a child or be a mother, and he would never understand her capacity for love and sacrifice. She revealed how proud she was that she could help me in such a dire moment and defended her actions.

"He has no right to judge. He's never had a family!" she proclaimed. Her defense of me and her actions surprised me. And when I remember how she fought for us, it moves me. As Jacqueline Rose observes in *Mothers* (2018), "Given voice, space, and time, motherhood can, and should, be one of the central means through which a historical moment reckons with itself" (p. 17). My understanding of my history has shifted—it took me years to recognize the effects of my mother's defense of me. The reckoning is in the regrets I carry with me. My mother's and mine.

• • •

Mom was fearless, and she was afraid. She was giving, and she was withholding. Because she was grounded, she could not comprehend my mood fluctuations and inability to cooperate. At a turning point, when I asked for financial help with college, an expensive private university where I had financed everything on my own, she advised me to quit and move home to "become a secretary or something." It did not matter that I had the highest grade point average in my class and had worked many jobs to get by. She thought I was chasing rainbows and reaching beyond my potential, and that was that. It turned into a violent argument, after which I ran away and made do with odd jobs. I did not revisit Georgia for four years. What was I thinking? We lost valuable time together.

Mom was life-smart, but she could not understand why I was not "normal" or somebody important who might impress her friends. She was a loving mother, but she was also absent. She was too protective, but she was also too permissive. She did not know how to handle my ambition and intellect, and she instead critiqued my beauty (as she saw it), what she believed was my best and most promising feature. However, my mother should have been a women's rights activist. She was not. Instead, she was a widowed mother of three. The rigid gender roles of her generation constrained her. My mother was, thus, a victim of her time. Yes, she was a victim of patriarchy, a victim like all women.

My mother also taught me to survive. I hope she appreciated my complicated mind at her end because she saw herself in me. She did not know how brilliant she was and never appreciated her children's talents. Unfortunately, she never held one of my books in her hands.

• • •

My best work is yet to come because I seek to escape the toxicity of society's expectations of women, those ideals from which my mother tried to shield me. However, my mother thrived in the patriarchal-mandated roles I have wanted to avoid. I am as confused by and ambivalent about her complexity and my upbringing now as I ever was. The complicated female characters I create, women who are neither good nor bad, echo my mother's experiences and the profound uncertainty she imbued in me. My Motherline is strong—Mom gave me as much to puzzle about as she took away. But her voice lingers.

References

Leloup, J.-Y. (2002). *The gospel of Mary Magdalene*. Inner Traditions.

Lowinsky, N. R. (1992). *The motherline*. Fisher King Press.

Plath, S. (1975). *Letters home by Sylvia Plath: Correspondence 1950–1963* (A. S. Plath, Ed.). Faber and Faber.

Rose, J. (2018). *Mothers: An essay on love and cruelty*. Farrar, Straus and Giroux.

Teresa of Ávila. (2008). *Interior castle* (E. A. Peers, Trans.). Dover Publications. (Original work published 1588)

CHAPTER 7

Wheel in the Sky

The most as you'll ever go/Is back where you used to know/If grown-ups could laugh this slow/Where as you watch the hour snow/Years may go by.

RICKIE LEE JONES, "On Saturday Afternoons in 1963"

• •
•

People strive to understand their memories by telling stories.

During the summer between my high school junior and senior years, I visited St. Augustine with my best friend, Marbrey. We were naïve and silly girls, monstrously invincible witmeisters in our fake I.D., sunbaked, ten-earrings-on-each-ear age. Marbrey had worked two jobs the previous school year to buy her clunker, an old 1970s LTD that *kathumped* in the heat. In June, we thudded Marbrey's Ford to Florida with the windows cranked down and a Journey cassette wailing on repeat in her newly installed stereo. We played the tape when we rode in her car. It was required. Marbrey, in her best second soprano, wailed her Steve Perry impersonations: *Wheel in the sky keeps on turnin'/I don't know where I'll be tomorrow.*

We were on the way to Marbrey's father's house, a suburban home with a kidney-shaped pool close to the beach, where we surfed all the best spots on the northern Atlantic coast (OK, we sunbathed on the beach and stalked the surfers). We partied at keggers each night and kissed tan lifeguards who never removed their sunglasses. The summer was the most fun I had ever had, but by early August, we had to get back to school, and on the drive home, we got lost.

• • •

The danger of one story is the danger of discarding one person's experience while amplifying another's. It is getting lost. Alas, focusing only on specific individuals can result in a single story of bigotry, lumping people into general classes and types. A solitary version of representation can lead to typecasting. In her 2009 lecture for TED conferences, *The Danger of a Single Story*, Chimamanda Adichie states, "The single story creates stereotypes, and the

© CATE MCGOWAN, 2025 | DOI:10.1163/9789004712379_007

problem with stereotypes is not that they are always untrue, but that they are always incomplete" (13:06). As Adichie points out, the danger of a sole narrative can also reinforce self-fulfilling immanence promulgated by the dominant class and "show[s] a people as one thing, as only one thing, over and over again, and that is what they become" (2009, 9:27). Yes, our society's preconceived notions of what defines a "story" are limiting at best.

The way to transform society and create safety in narratives is individuation—we must tell our unique stories. Of course, we all think we should fit in or be "normal." This driving need for assimilation might underscore an acceptance of white normativity. Since childhood, society has impressed on us how there is a "right way" to exist and how the white male Western perspective is the only perspective. This dominance proliferates. Our language shapes our ideas and how we gain knowledge. People understand texts and stories differently depending on their worldviews and perspectives. It makes sense that our communication choices influence others and construct and deepen social, cultural, geographical, and historical understanding.

• • •

A renewal of interest in storytelling theories, specifically those highlighted by feminist literary critics and authors, including work by Ursula K. Le Guin, contributes to defining writing style innovations. Le Guin, Donna Haraway, and Anna Tsing. In Le Guin's chapbook, *The Carrier Bag Theory of Fiction*, first published in 1986 (1986/2019), she begins with the familiar story of the "Ascent of Man," a fable framing the origins of humanity, a hunting epic with a male hero, a linear narrative relayed countless times throughout history concludes with goals reached and hopes dashed, a mixed plot of triumph and tragedy. Le Guin argues that these stories forget how the first humans were hunter-*gatherers*, noting that the gathering role was the most important for societies, a sustainable aspect of survival (1986/2019, p. 25). It does not take a hero to pick berries, but foraging for food and other objects needed for sustenance allows for much free time, including time to tell stories. Le Guin proposes that a carrier bag was more valuable than a weapon in prehistoric societies (1986/2019, p. 30). It is also a better narrative model than the linear arrow or spear. The straight arrow is one possibility (a chronological approach), whereas the carrier bag can hold many other options (Le Guin, 1986/2019, p. 36).

Le Guin, therefore, posits a different tale—the "Ascent of Woman." In her imaginary East European country, Orsinia, she explores matriarchal narratives in *Orsinian Tales* (1976/2004) and a novel, *Malafrena* (1979/1980). In places like contemporary Earth societies, the stories depict the historical dominance of men. The narrators, females, have been telling stories in the land since ancient times. Le Guin's characters gather food and share their tales, but never write these narratives. Compared to men's linear and goal-driven records, the open-ended tales told by Le Guinian women are more resistant to tyranny.

• • •

The route back to Atlanta for Marbrey and me was simple: an eight-hour shot overnight. We were on the highway by 9:00 P.M., our bare feet gripping the dash; gallons of Coca-Cola and the adrenaline of recounting our summer gallivants fueled us. Halfway home, after zooming through the darkness across red-clay expanses of South Georgia, forks of lightning fractured the black sky. Marbrey and I pointed in amazement as another staggering display of light flashed, the bright, jagged lines ripping across the horizon.

"Did you see that one? ... There's *another*!" We got lost as we chased the lightning, driving toward the middle of the storm and ignoring where we were going. We soon forgot to sing, and when we exited off I-75, it was my turn to drive. Regardless of how I floored it, the clouds still billowed out of reach on the horizon. We meandered on rural back roads until the lightning vanished, and the sky turned lavender in the early morning.

• • •

To elicit change and prevent cultural "single stories," we must ask critical questions: Who inhabits our stories? Where do our stories take place? Why do stories exist in this world? Must a story be factual, or can it stretch the truth? How do we know that what we are reading/writing/listening to is indeed a story?

Contrary to Adichie's important and utterly valid contention, my story is singular. And there *is* a single story, at least on the macro level. It is one of humanity. The best stories I read are by people I will never meet, by authors composing narratives in different locales or times, relaying their experiences so realistically with such relatable details I can suspend disbelief as if the events were happening to me in the moments I am poring through a book. Yes, we all are living one narrative. *Life* is a single story. The human experience, at its most basic emotional level, is singular. And I empathize when I read—I understand a person better when I read their story.

We are each adding chapters to this universal tale of empathy. All of us have so much in common. The basics apply—each story has a beginning, middle, and end; we are all born, struggle to survive through our time here on Earth, and die. Some of us have families, but we were all children. And we will (hopefully) all grow old (readers age by the second as they read each word on a page). Yes, each person's experience is exceptional, but no writer is an auteur. All authors are the products of a community fostering the creator's development and stories. The moral is that our tales can be different, valid, *and* similar: "When we reject the single story, when we realize that there is never a single story about any place, we regain a kind of paradise" (Adichie, 2009, 18:22). No single story can fully grasp the significance of living in this world, but we all share so many lived experiences.

• • •

Social scientist Anna Tsing relays a tale in *The Mushroom at the End of the World*, using remembrance to highlight the importance of perspective in storytelling and how various micro-stories comprise the macro-story: "One value of keeping precarity in mind is that it makes us remember that changing circumstances is the stuff of survival" (2015, p. 27). Tsing says the future is uncertain and frightening, but storytelling can help us cope and face what is to come. By listening to a tale, the audience can vicariously place herself in the narrator's position and imagine herself in the future, remembering herself in the past. An act of remembrance contextualizes present views and arouses change. Tsing argues how, in the modern era, the Anthropocene has brought about the need for novel forms of remembrance and storytelling to help people cope with unpredictability and constant shifts in the *Zeitgeist*. Thus, stories help us shift our thinking, inspiring us to enact transformation to social structures rather than succumbing to any fatalistic notions that we have no control over our fates or can no longer alter the world. With this idea of recollection, the mandate for feminist scholars shifts: Tell stories of alternative realities and open-ended reports resistant to the tyranny of humans, especially paternalistic cultures.

Another Le Guinian "carrying" trait of modern-era storytelling is its emphasis on empathy, as Donna Haraway highlights in *Staying with the Trouble: Making Kin in the Chthulucene* (2016). She rightly claims that our discrete, different worlds characterize our existences. Each storyteller constructs their place in the language of their existence. Storytellers can invent stories as fabricated places: "We are obligated to speak from situated worlds, but we no longer need to start from a humanist patriline and its breath-taking erasures and high-wire acts" (Haraway, 2016, p. 132). Someone's story, therefore, may shift our views. Haraway proposes how a carrier bag can contain many levels of narratives, and the reader can collect multiple worlds into one account and create new ones by understanding herself in correlation with others (2016, pp. 7, 125). Readers must relate to two worlds: the story's settings and their own. The reader must engage with the narrative and interpret the account in the physical world. As a result, the reader is accountable to others. Reading never happens in a vacuum, but is a conversation of civic experience between readers and writers who are equal partners.

Contemporary theories of storytelling, whether feminist in theme or derived from Postmodernism, suggest it is not enough to pronounce a story's factual basis. Instead, we should assert that a story is fiction only sometimes. When we declare that a tale in its completed incarnation is untrue only sometimes, we pressure readers to digest a story open to interpretation. This expectation is unfair. The carrier bag story employs the notion of an everyday object often overlooked, challenging readers to examine the object of a narrative for what it is, inspect its physical characteristics, and explore the historical reasons for its popularity. It is a story that challenges us to think about the materiality of storytelling and how narratives affect our lives.

A carrier bag toting stories becomes its own kind of story, one of interpretation: Reading is a hermeneutic or revelatory act. We interpret society and a fictional universe through stories, influencing how we interpret the world.

• • •

At dawn, after never catching the lightning storm, Marbrey and I visited her old hometown by chance. She insisted we were close enough to see the house where she lived before her parents broke up. "What if we don't find it," she said.

I could relate. Marbrey's story was like mine. We had experienced loss and death in our immediate families, and returning to a time and place where we had been happy was impossible, but there we were, at her childhood home, where things had been better.

After driving through Morocco and Iceland to get there, we found Marbrey's old street and house. It was 6:00 A.M. We turned onto the municipality's main road lined by looming oaks—country-town Georgia-on-a-postcard. We parked along the curb beside a cracked sidewalk.

"It's smaller than I remember," she said as she inspected the mansion from the passenger seat. To my eye, from our position on the street, it was a brick goliath flanked by tall columns peeling their paint. Marbrey whispered, "Let me get out and look for a minute."

I opened the door, stretched my legs, and quietly edged it shut. Marbrey and I tip-toed to the gate through the morning dew.

"I recognize all of this," she said as we peered over the iron fence. The home had no lights shining inside. The curtains were drawn. "I'm going closer?" I joked with her.

"OK, but if a dog comes and bites you, I'm not helping. I'm running." Marbrey did not laugh—she was already deep in her memories as she tugged open the cranky gate. She crouched and ran her hand over the inset stones on the concrete steps. The terraced front yard sloped down to the river, its arena of hedges thick with shadows, and magnolia trees towered above the wraparound porch.

I thought of my house. Our front lawn is where my only intact photo was taken—a group snapshot someone took a month before my dad died. It is in my desk drawer today. I am unsure who snapped the picture, but all five of us pose on the green lawn in front of a bank of pink azaleas in the bright spring sun. We are wearing our Sunday best, my sister and me in pale blue Swiss-dot dresses, my brother tugging at a clip-on tie. In the now-yellowed snapshot, we are all squinting, and I am in front, half-crouching, hugging my beloved dog Frisky. My dad is laughing. His mouth is half-open. My mom is embarrassed or pleased; I cannot tell.

I often reflect on that day before my life went south.

In the quiet dawn, while sitting on the steps of her childhood home, Marbrey's voice wobbled. "I-I guess nothing's ever as good as it was when we were kids, huh?" I patted her back as she tucked her head between her tanned knees and cried.

"Yeah, life sucks," was all I could say. But she knew I understood.

For a few more minutes, we sat together in silence. And Marbrey's despair and memories became mine. Our stories were different, sure, yet they were also the same, somehow inextricably intertwined. We had lived through similar terrible childhoods. And if we had not, I would have known her story anyway. Empathy and emotional truth bonded us.

Marbrey and I held hands as we stood and walked back to her old car. And we drove away in silence toward Atlanta.

Instead of getting lost, we found the lightning.

References

Adichie, C. N. (2009). *The danger of the single story* [Video]. Retrieved March 23, 2024, from https://www.ted.com/talks/chimamanda_adichie_the_danger_ of_a_single_story?language=en

Haraway, D. (2016). *Staying with the trouble: Making kin in the Chthulucene.* Duke University Press.

Journey. (1977). Wheel in the sky. On *On Infinity* [MP3].

Le Guin, U. K. (1980). *Malafrena.* Berkley Books. (Original work published 1979)

Le Guin, U. K. (2004). *Orsinian tales*. Perennial. (Original work published 1976)

Le Guin, U. K. (2019). *The carrier bag theory of fiction*. Ignota Books. (Original work published 1986)

Tsing, A. L. (2015). *The mushroom at the end of the world: On the possibility of life in capitalist ruins*. Princeton University Press.

CHAPTER 8

Writing Is Revision

As the Tibetan Buddhist nun and writer Pema Chödrön points out in *The Places That Scare You* (2002), there is no fixed point in existence, only a continuum, an "approach reflect[ing] what are called the three noble principles: good in the beginning, good in the middle, good at the end. They can be used in all the activities of our lives" (p. 1). Whenever I write, I dread the first step, thinking, *This could be the most dangerous piece I'll ever write!* After many years of facing this kind of anxiety, I trust I will push through the fear and dig in to perceive the "essence of the fearless, open state of mind" (Chödrön, 2002, p. 103). I compose through terror. My places of fear are my feelings.

I am terrified because I cannot control life's happenings and outcomes. So, I write because I can manage *this* story I am telling now. The beginning of a story provides me with endless possibilities. There is hope for a positive outcome. Though my path narrows in the middle of writing, I can shift directions flexibly and affect the conclusion. No matter how a piece ends, I appreciate the gift of closure and the opportunity to begin again. But I also write because it is my way of accepting imperfections. After all, my writing is a work in progress; it is never complete.

I must confront my demons. As feminist literary theorist Hélène Cixous exhorts in *Three Steps on the Ladder of Writing*, "The only book that is worth writing is the one we don't have the courage or strength to write. The book that hurts us (we who are writing), that makes us tremble, redden, bleed" (1993, p. 32). However, unfinished business is not what worries me. What frightens me most? Dying. I cannot control or know how I will die in the way I can manage this page through sheer force of will. Yet I must accept because death will happen. And I will never be "done" with my work. Acceptance is the way forward through this fear. Often, I contemplate how the dead are unaware they have reached an end. If we possess an awareness when we pass and believe living beings have souls and are cognizant, we will not care when we go. We are gone. Science is certainty: Matter shifts form and converts into energy.

• • •

Words are hard. Yes, I know I am using peculiar diction here—I should say, "Writing is difficult." I enjoy presenting words and compositions as unyielding surfaces, so there is no reason to revise or change my simple, albeit grammatically questionable, statement. And writing from an emotional stance (*pathos*) is the most difficult compositional approach to navigate. Yes, it *is* hard to bear one's soul with creative nonfiction. However, I suffer less when writing fiction—I can distance myself from the final product because the stories are untrue. Or are they? The creative nonfiction gig, however, is brutal from beginning to end.

Writing has been a painful endeavor during the last few years, dredging up issues I hoped to bury. In a couple of newer essays, I revisited a long time ago when someone sexually assaulted me. In another piece, I paid tribute to my best friend, who died of cancer. After I thought I was done, I re-read the work within hours of hatching it. With both pieces, I found my words lacking. So, I walked back and revised them. And I ultimately deleted them. An erasure of my mistakes and my raw feelings. If only I could also erase painful memories that stick with me.

•••

Years ago, I met with a group of writers who sat Quaker-style in meditation before we began generative exercises.[1] The group had invited a visitor, a Chiricahua Apache traditional healer who introduced himself as Iron Eagle. Deep gullies etched his cheeks. He was old. He told us to sit in a circle as he intimated, "Everything's a circle; everything's linked." I hoped to tap into something divine as I moved into formation.

I tried to relax and open myself to the experience with Iron Eagle.

There are never satisfying shortcuts. No one can help me travel my path.

Iron Eagle spoke as he jabbed his short finger at a hand-held drum, pointing to the four painted sections on the instrument's skin: "These four sections represent my beliefs. All connected." A cross divided the quadrants, with each section a distinct color: yellow, red, black, white; fire, water, earth, air; North, South, East, West.

He explained the sun, sky, his tribe's animal totems, and how humans are one family. My mind wandered to my totems. When Iron Eagle reached the water section on his drum's wheel, I pictured the ponds and lakes I had paddled across or visited.

He said, "Water has its own memory."

My thoughts drifted as Iron Eagle explained the profound connection between earth and air. I contemplated water's whims and how liquids seek their own level and remembered Pascal's principle: Through fluids, pressure spreads uniformly, and the air above the surface supplies this pressure (OpenStax, 2022).

The drum beat pulled me deeper into my memories, and a childhood experiment sprang to mind: I assembled a network of tubes on a table, some vertical and others horizontal, all interconnected at various heights and lengths. I connected multiple hoses to a spigot, aimed them into the tubes' openings, and turned on the water. Despite the height differences, the water rose uniformly in each tube, defying my expectations with its synchronized ascent. As I sat there, science told me a story, revealing the secrets of water's behavior. Pascal and his pressure principles, the fluid ballet in plumbing, and the childhood experiment are all magical, interconnected threads. I traveled the depths of my memories and pictured my father's tools in our basement, the levels he used to ensure the flush installation of shelves or the paintings he hung. Those levels were never wrong; their glass inserts with acid-green liquid and an air bubble between black indicator lines ran parallel to the ground beneath us. My father often said an object's levels were "true" if the level's bubble floated in the center. "True" sounded better than "right"—there is strength in the term "true."

"We're all composed of water," Iron Eagle reminded us, his voice draping over my wandering ideas. *Yes,* I thought, *I'm more than half water and seek my own level. I'm "true."*

The world teems with metaphors. No, the world is a metaphor, my existence a waking dream. Water knows where to go. I encounter it in various stages, and those meetings are short compared to the entire journey of liquid entering my home and flowing back into the earth. If I go to the tap and turn on the spigot, I only discern a moment of water's existence. It has traveled to me through pipes over hundreds of miles; it reaches me when I need it, streaming through pipes above my head in the attic, down into a kitchen faucet, a steady stream I can filter between my fingers. The miracle of water swirls down the drain and disappears, escaping from where it came. It is here in my world for only seconds. Its history and future are beyond estimation, but the moment of now in my consciousness is finite. The moment I need it, it comes to me when I beckon.

• • •

This section is roughly the middle of the essay, and I'm more confident as I write it. Does it make sense?

The worst part about death is the stuff the earth-departed leaves behind. There, in the aftermath, is a dead member's collateral damage. The departed leave their friends behind, people who might remember notes passed in third grade or letters sent from Greece during a wild summer; mothers or sons might obsess over a last desperate, pleading phone call; the dead abandon pets left hungry and forgotten in dark apartments. The dead will never again yell a favorite swear word or laugh at a good joke. Regular routes through the woods will grow over. Baristas might notice the absent friendly customer who waited patiently for double foam. Both minor and significant traces will evaporate, and soon, the memories of those who passed will dim, with only a few peaks highlighted on the graph of a receding life. Soon, those who remember will be gone, too.

• • •

Writing is revision. I no longer have a blog because I cannot leave well enough alone—a live essay is an invitation to disaster. Our quick-as-a-nanosecond-cyber-society requires writers to reveal all, tell all NOW, so we race to add our two cents in public forums before our ideas are well-rounded. And when we discover errors in our posts, we hurry to revise what we have shared. Revising a piece that remains visible as we make changes is stressful.

Why? When I park my writing online, anyone can read it anytime. Mopping up a mess under a tight deadline adds pressure. Each second ticking away on the analog clock is a second someone has read my shitty eighth draft published on the blog.

I must come clean about those blog essays that I no longer write. Most were problematic as soon as I hit "publish." After many repairs and revamps (Word-Press showed I drafted a particular essay 46 times after I posted), they are copacetic, sure, but not outstanding, and, of course, never perfect. These days, I can live with the off-line work I have written and all my in-process compositions because no one is reading them.

Later, I might peruse a piece I thought was acceptable when I wrote it. I will catch it differently in my writer's ear and think it is a disaster with egregious citation omissions or clunky wording. But I am never safe if someone has already read my online material. That is why I hide most of my pieces and why submitting my work for publication is difficult. I doubt what I produce and share, my sentences, words, and what I have put on the page.

When my work appears in print, I encounter a new level of personal scrutiny. After a literary magazine accepts a piece of mine, I have one shot at proofing the galleys—this was the case with my book of short stories. Unless there is a significant reprint, the author is stuck with what the publisher sews or pastes into a book's spine when it goes to the printing press.

If my excellent editor has been attentive to details and catches errors, more power to them and the work—I will trust my stories or poems will stand the test of time. However, my collection has an error I long to rectify. I spelled "Polaroid" as "Polaraid." I also had talented editors for my flash story in Norton's *Flash Fiction International*, but that was not enough. The galleys arrived on time, and I dove into my final proof, penciling an edit, revising "were" to "was," and changing the subjunctive mood to the indicative. It is a significant grammatical error, and the editors did not catch the gaffe. And so, with a glaring mood boo-boo, my story sits alongside creations by legendary authors—Kafka, Kawabata, and Keret. It is there for folks to read. I guess people could say I am neurotic. I think I am.

Recently, an extraordinarily successful writer, a close author friend, confessed to me that he had found errors in his novel, a text shortlisted for the National Book Award. My friend discovered the errors only after his book went to print twenty-one years ago. He sounded relieved when he intimated he had corrected the book's faults when it was going through a reprint in honor of his newest novel, another nominee for the prestigious literary award. I may need to take a chill pill if a two-time National Book Award finalist feels this way about his fiction.

There is a danger with never-ending revision, however. Social media and blog posts? We can delete or revise what we have shared. We can re-furl whatever freak flags we have hoisted up the social media flagpole, and I hope no one has screenshotted a flawed revelation for posterity's sake. For my more "serious" work saved in word-processed files, I tweak with abandon, but in changing and shifting any piece, I risk the original text losing its zing. I often murder my pieces when I hasten the process, never truly letting a work rest until I have worked through it.

• • •

In 2012, in the Sanctuary of Mercy church in Borja, Spain, an older parishioner named Cecilia Giménez took it upon herself to revive a faded and flaking fresco of Jesus titled *Ecce Homo* (Behold the Man) painted in 1930 by Elías García Martínez. Unfortunately, Giménez's restoration resulted in a drastically altered face of Jesus. People widely recognized and comically dubbed the unintentional transformation of the painting as "Ecce Mono" (Behold the Monkey). The incident gained global attention, sparking discussions about art preservation and the unintended consequences of amateur restoration efforts (Minder, 2012).

I am often enthusiastic as I revise my creations, aiming to enhance my work's impact. However, balancing my intent with improving the original iteration takes work. Inexperience leads to revisions made without careful consideration and could distort meaning or tone. Writers must, therefore, approach the revision process carefully, ensuring that each change contributes to a work's overall improvement, much as a skilled restorer delicately enhances an artwork without diminishing its core identity.

Yes, we can over-edit and beat the passion out of a piece so it no longer resembles its original form. I keep thinking of older movie stars' botched plastic surgeries, a more pedestrian example than one of a fresco; an actor appears a shadow of his original self with a misshapen nose and angled cheekbones. I am uninterested in composing plastic surgery prose or verse, shifting the piece so much, muddying words, and losing sight of my intention. A significant amount of my work has improved over time through many revisions. Indeed, I have improved my essays, enhancing them beyond their original published form. I am mortified that readers might have trudged or suffered through my developing work. If only I could contact each reader and say, *Hey, this piece is better now*. Or, *I am in a better place now. I'm a better person.*

• • •

During our writing group meeting, Iron Eagle pounded his drum. He asked us to close our eyes, though I had already closed mine. He then pounded out a heartbeat. *Bum-ba-bum, bum-ba-bum.*

I was calm, and my anxiety dissipated.

Iron Eagle sang, "Light. Our hearts." With my eyes clamped shut, Iron Eagle's voice drew me in, and I pictured his hand opening into a budding blossom, the daylight tumbling from the window, tatting patterns lace onto my palm. With my eyes closed, I eyed a puddle of water trickling into the soil beneath the building, penetrating the concrete foundations. A torrent wrapped around plateau bases and gushed below clay mountains; underground water streamed through the sacredness of animal and plant remains, of humans dead for countless years; waves rushed past decayed, forgotten scribes farther down into musky soil, deeper still through bedrock. The water coursed into the Earth's molten core, converting to steam, and as it reached this transformation, the vapor rose and returned to me. It weaved around and over, above and under all of us in the room, wrapping us in a net. We were one.

Yes, and my creativity is a metaphor aiming for immortality. I opened myself to the dream, and Iron Eagle began playing a song on his flute, a furtive wail bringing me back to the circle.

• • •

Those left here in the moments after a death carry dense stones in their guts; they must clean after someone dies—cancel phone accounts, contact acquaintances, plan funerals, and pay those last bills before the power is cut. Those left behind must clean up. This tidying is emotional, too, of course. But we all live with it each day. We are warriors.

I am a clerk who records my words and acts, and the meaning-making will die with me one day. It is necessary to ensure others remember, so I play my part. Yes, others will forget me, but I accept this inevitability as I type each word toward peace.

These words are close to the end of my essay, and I'm grateful I made it. I'm terrified of writing once more. But I will. Yes, I believe in words. The correct combination of sentences and paragraphs is a spell or an incantation. My words might fire readers' synapses; they could shift paradigms. If I do it right (write), the reader and I might connect on a karmic level. Writing is difficult. Better said, words are hard—like a rock upside the head.

Note

1   Segments about Iron Eagle in this essay are adapted from my article, "Water Has Its Own Memory," originally published in the *Peace and Justice Initiative Bi-Annual Newsletter* (McGowan, 2015b).

References

Chödrön, P. (2002). *The places that scare you: A guide to fearlessness in difficult times.* Shambhala Classics.

Cixous, H. (1993). *Three steps on the ladder of writing* (S. Cornell & S. Sellers, Trans.). Columbia University Press. (Original work published 1990).

McGowan, C. (2015). Water has its own memory. *Peace and Justice Initiative Bi-Annual Newsletter, 6*(1), 7–8.

Minder, R. (2012, August 24). Despite good intentions, a fresco in Spain is ruined. *New York Times.* Retrieved March 28, 2024, from https://proxy1.library.jhu.edu/login?url=https://www.proquest.com/newspapers/despite-good-intentions-fresco-spain-is-ruined/docview/1034805066/se-2?accountid=11752 https://catalyst.library.jhu.edu/openurl/01JHU_INST/01JHU_INST:JHU?&genre=article&issn=03624331&title=Despite+Good+Intentions%2C+A+Fresco+in+Spain+Is+Ruined&volume=&issue=&date=2012&atitle=Despite+Good+Intentions%2C+A+Fresco+in+Spain+Is+Ruined%3A+%5BForeign+Desk%5D&spage=A.4&sid=ProQ%3Anytimes&author=Minder

OpenStax. (2022). *14.5: Pascal's Principle and Hydraulics.* Libretexts. Retrieved March 23, 2024 from https://phys.libretexts.org/Bookshelves/University_Physics/University_Physics_(OpenStax)/Book%3A_University_Physics_I_-_Mechanics_Sound_Oscillations_and_Waves_(OpenStax)/14%3A_Fluid_Mechanics/14.05%3A_Pascal's_Principle_and_Hydraulics

CHAPTER 9

Negative Capability

As I neared the end of drafting my doctoral dissertation, I sailed through with the approbation of my committee members, basking in the compliments and interesting questions directed at my text—I had an answer for each query. But at my dissertation defense, all was not well. The only man on my committee spoke up, and I almost heard a record skip, like when everything goes terribly wrong in a movie. The male committee member questioned my thesis, noting I had never explicitly defined patriarchy or explained how women writing their truths might challenge the existing order. My explications were in the manuscript if he had bothered to read it.

The women on the committee were aghast, eyes wide with disbelief. I stammered, responding as best I could, but I never needed to prove patriarchy exists. It is an empirical truth; the man's behavior proved it. Patriarchy does not need defining, but I will explain it here in my terms.

We women live with patriarchy at each moment of our lives. Male domination has shaped our lives. From what we eat, speak, and act to how we think and form world opinions. Many male theorists have never understood how women must move through their environment and navigate language to find a means of expressing feminine individuality.

•••

Sigmund Freud traffics in the notion that humans have access to or attempt recognition of empirical truth. However, Jacques Lacan, in "The Mirror-Phase" (1949/2005), questions notions of self and truth, exploring how linguistic and ideological structures shape our ideas through consciousness and unconsciousness. Freud's ego, super-ego, and id from "The Ego and the Id" (1923/1995) are riding along in Lacan's ideas, but do they sit in the front seat?

Our instincts often control us, irrespective of how much we can pinpoint the impetus for our actions. The brain's limbic system is the older "mammalian" sensitivity controlling our instinctive feelings, contrasted with the rational part of our brain, where we think we control our behaviors. This internal discourse occurs within the aspects of our consciousness where we can experience our various socially constructed identities working as Jungian archetypes (Jung, 1938/2005) and the Lacanian "I." But men, haughty males sitting on dissertation committees, predetermined these roles.

© CATE MCGOWAN, 2025 | DOI:10.1163/9789004712379_009

Our choices during our discrete journeys are fraught with mistakes or challenges where the id may play a more significant role, contrasted with the super-
ego's position. As we grow older and accumulate more experiences informing
our actions, the super-ego plays a more substantial role as a stabilizing wisdom. Similarly, Lacan presupposes a mirror phase as "the symbolic matrix in
which the I is precipitated in a primordial form, before it is objectified in the
dialectic of identification with the other, and before language restores to it, in
the universal, its function as subject" (1949/2005, p. 621).

When I initially read Lacan's "Mirror State," I remembered Virginia Woolf's
A Room of One's Own (1929). Woolf investigates an "I," though differently
than the singular first-person pronoun Lacan features. In Room, Woolf's narrator interrogates a villainous character, a masculine "I," whom she reads in
a make-believe book. Woolf's narrator has difficulty interpreting beyond the
villain's dominant male signifier of "I":

> But after reading a chapter or two [of the fictional male narrator's story],
> a shadow seemed to lie across the page. It was a straight dark bar, a
> shadow shaped something like the letter "I." One began dodging this way
> and that to catch a glimpse of the landscape behind it. ... Back one was
> always hailed to the letter "I." One began to be tired of the "I." ... I turned a
> page or two, looking for something or other—the worst of it's that in the
> shadow of the letter "I," all is shapeless as mist. Is that a tree? No, it is a
> woman. (1929/2002, pp. 83–84)

Woolf's narrator expresses infuriation, addressing women's subordination and
forced complicity as subjects, objects, and, yes, readers. She questions how
society constructs females and their activities as inferior. Yes, culture displaces
women and hides them in the shadows (if they are not being gazed upon as
objects). In a masculine-constructed narrative structure, such as Freud and
Lacan's, men often only include women as outsiders or subjects of a story, not
creators. This diminishment and second-class status for women is patriarchy
undermining any feminine attempts at equality.

How depressing.

•••

My academic work explores historical and contemporary theories addressing
creativity's source, nature, and development. The spirit of innovation understood through the eyes of creative individuals and the lenses of eminent theorists, philosophers, and researchers helps me to know myself. In many literary

works I write or critique, I focus on coming of age, specifically studying the nascence of artists. The *Künstlerroman* is rich with potential as it tries to reveal the creative process and the cultures from which creations form. In this book of essays, I have attempted the same revelations. Of course, my work is not James Joyce's *Portrait of the Artist as a Young Man* or John Barth's *Lost in the Funhouse*, but I understand how my nonfiction tries to both mystify *and* de-mystify authorship similar to what Joyce and Barth were aiming to do. To connect my creative and critical work to any concrete steps of creativity, I examine and note the similarities between Graham Wallas, Eudora Welty, and Malcolm Cowley, whose ideas ground me and provide me with an understanding of my creative process.

While I do not subscribe to compartmentalizing or classifying steps of creative processes, in Wallas's tome, he does an outstanding job tracing how creativity happens. Wallas highlights the progression of creation along a continuum, the subtle symbiosis of conscious and unconscious thinking creators experience. He examines the "success ... in thought[,] ... the creation of something felt to be beautiful and true rather than the solution of a prescribed problem" (Wallas, 1926, p. 82). By breaking down creativity into "the four stages of Preparation, Incubation, Illumination, and Verification," Wallas provides a rough blueprint for identification (1926, p. 82).

During Wallas's Preparation stage, potential avenues of creation are "investigated ... in all directions" (1926, p. 80). Innovative ideas germinate from this accrual of reserves, and the creator is aware of this groundwork's combination of learning, research, and framing *in situ* (Wallas, 1926, p. 81). After Preparation, Incubation takes hold—a period of unplanned gestation, and during this second stage, a creator exerts no direct effort. Wallas notes how the Incubation stage entails embracing oppositions—the "negative fact" to avoid deliberation; the "positive fact" enacted through a sequence of instinctive moves (or, as he terms the condition, the "foreconscious" and "forevoluntary") (1926, p. 86). He states:

> Voluntary abstention from conscious thought on any problem may take two forms: the period of abstention may be spent either in conscious mental work on other problems or in a relaxation from all conscious mental work. The first kind of Incubation economizes time and is therefore often the better. (Wallas, 1926, p. 86)

If I let ideas rest, they may blossom when I return to them with a fresh mind.

Wallas, therefore, suggests a method of improving Incubation's benefits. He believes in the importance of deliberately interrupting concentrated effort: "We can often get more results in the same way by beginning several problems in succession, and voluntarily leaving them unfinished while we turn to others than by finishing our work on each problem at one sitting" (Wallas, 1926, p. 86). Thus, for Wallas, letting a problem or issue percolate is preferable to active rumination.

The Illumination stage follows Incubation in Wallas's schema, where he draws on "sudden illumination." This third stage features an epiphany, a state an aware person cannot force, a state the subliminal mind welcomes when all elements coalesce during the Preparation and Incubation stages. In Illumination, disparate ideas combine to reveal a new way forward for a creator. Nevertheless, Wallas warns against forcing Illumination: "[T]he final 'flash,' or 'click' ... is the culmination of a successful train of association, which may have lasted for an appreciable time, and which has probably been preceded by a series of tentative and unsuccessful trains" (1926, pp. 93–94). In Wallas's progression, Illumination is a marriage of all elements leading to a *Eureka!* moment, a condition that Preparation and Incubation anticipate.

Unlike Wallas's middle two stages, the last stage, Verification, parallels Preparation as a deliberate effort to test an idea's validity. However, more critical in Verification is that it lays bare the concomitance of stages. None of the four steps is discrete; the innovation apparatus is in flux, and each part informs the other. Wallas contends:

> In the daily stream of thought, these four different stages constantly overlap each other as we explore different problems. ... And it must always be remembered that much very important thinking ... resembles musical composition in that the stages leading to success are not very easily fitted into a "problem and solution" scheme. (1926, pp. 81–82)

The stages of creativity blend and inform one another on a continuum. They are not necessarily sequential but recursive, recalling Barth's *Lost in the Funhouse*, which lays bare the adolescent protagonist, Ambrose, who is on the cusp of becoming an engaged and aware artist who replays moments of his life often: "[He] ... seemed unable to forget the least detail of his life" (2006, p. 78).

• • •

Cloud formations fascinated the English painter John Constable, who fretted he had "failed to 'show' the world that it is possible to accomplish" the lush landscapes he witnessed and the mercurial clouds he desperately wanted to represent (Hamilton, 2022, p. 362). Constable painted hundreds of studies of clouds in his time, and his subject matter allowed for his own and his viewers'

interpretations—loose abstract renderings of the sky. The artist never was satisfied he had effectively rendered the radiance he witnessed in real life:

> I know very well what I am about, and that my skies have not been
> neglected, though they have often failed in execution, no doubt, from an
> over-anxiety about them which will alone destroy that easy appearance
> which nature always has in all her movements. (Leslie, 1896, p. 104)

Constable's frustration at his inability to capture the majesty of English skies is
understandable, but I propose that writers accept that we will never replicate
our experiences. We can devise new ones, however.

I am an Aquarius, a veritable cloud in the astrological world. A water bearer.
And water is a miracle, how it evaporates, rising to the sky to form clouds. The
remaining elements on *Terra firma* are leaden and struck with gravity. But not
water; it overcomes immanence. So why is it a negative characterization to
describe states of mind as "cloudy"? After all, the necessary stuff emanates
from clouds. Drinking water. Drizzle. Electric thunder. Clouds shift and transform, become something, and metamorphose in shape and size.

In recent years, the usual murky cloud I walk through has darkened. I do
not know where I am going. Clarion perception, too much awareness, can be
as detrimental as obliviousness. I find tremendous ideas when I do not over-
think and dive into a project when I silence my inner critic. People overrate
self-knowledge and self-reflection. Soberly viewing the world's problems is so
discouraging that it might deter creativity and the writing life.

Keats wrote in 1817 in praise of a rare creative faculty. He called it "Negative
Capability," which is "when man is capable of being in uncertainties, Mysteries
[*sic*], doubts, without any irritable reaching after fact & reason" (para. 13). This
state happens when artists know how to allow their most captivating inner
selves to shine through, leaving their unconsciousness to work unresolved,
allowing unknowns. Negative capability is embracing mystery, not knowing
the ending, but being open to other angles. Painting clouds. Navigating *through*
clouds.

• • •

It is strange how years of writing labor have altered my perceptions. Decades
ago, when I read Eudora Welty's memoir, *One Writer's Beginnings*, I thought,
*Well, these are the ruminations of a successful old writer from a different era. She
really cannot teach me anything.* I was wrong, naïve. In reacquainting myself
with Welty's life, my formative experiences closely align with hers. After over

thirty years of dedicating my time to writing, I have a newfound admiration for Welty's novels and short stories because I can relate to her "beginnings" and correlate those experiences with Wallas's four stages of creativity outlined in *The Art of Thought*. Indeed, Wallas's steps provide an excellent springboard for examining Welty's explanations of incipient authorship.

Welty's development, described in *One Writer's Beginnings*, echoes how Wallas defines creativity in *The Art of Thought*. Her book features three sections: "Listening," "Learning to See," and "Finding a Voice." In her first section, Welty explains how attendant listening acuity accompanies her vivid childhood memories and observations. She tells her readers how discussions and conversations she overheard inform her story's scenes, providing her with "stratagems and jokes and tricks and dares" (Welty, 1983/2020, p. 20). Welty reveals her extraordinary powers of perception in the memoir's second section, a perception as necessary as listening to the world and how she stores information. Welty describes this consciousness of her burgeoning authorship in childhood as a process of groundwork and cultivation, echoing Wallas's Preparation and Incubation stages: "Childhood's learning is made up of moments" (1983/2020, p. 9). Yes, Welty's "seeing" is comparable to Wallas's stage of "illumination," a word with multiple definitions. However, the definition here is "lighting up," the ability to grope out of darkness.

In expressing her Illumination stage, Welty recalls vivid scenes from her life, including family automobile excursions that later inspired "Death of a Traveling Salesman" (1983/2020, p. 117), explaining how the memory helped her create her protagonist and choreograph his movements. In "Finding a Voice," the last section of *One Writer's*, Welty clarifies how she incorporated years of experiencing the world into her work (1983/2020, p. 117). Her ideas about composing stories resemble Wallas's final stage, Verification. Only through the previous steps of listening and seeing, of Preparation, Incubation, and Illumination, does Welty reach the Verification stage, where she discovers her voice and tests the validity of the confluence of her ideas. Though she declares her characterizations are not autobiographical, she contends a "writer is in part all of his characters" (Welty, 1983/2020, p. 137)—this aligns with the *Künstlerroman* ideas I propound. And it aligns with my writing practice. Therefore, a writer vivifies a feeling and enters a character's "skin, heart, mind, and soul" (Welty, 1983/2020, p. 135).

Welty's most striking echoes of Wallas occur when she describes her process as fluid as she discusses separate journeys' convergences of times and places, believing people remember most deeply when they experience change or difference. Similarly, each iteration of Ambrose in *Life in the Funhouse* discovers himself when he travels. Welty's excursions inform her fiction: "[T]rips changed something in my life, each made its particular revelation" (1983/2020,

p. 92). Her accumulated knowledge becomes a source of revelation, and events follow a "continuous thread of revelation" (Welty, 1983/2020, p. 92). This continuous thread echoes Wallas's conception of creativity stages, which are not siloed but inform the other steps in no sequence.

But writing is not all about transcription or translation. It is about communicating ideas. As writers, we often feel frustrated because we rarely discover elegant ways to convey a concept perfectly, structure a novel seamlessly, or compose a revelatory poem. Yes, we search for a fix, a cure-all, the latest gimmick. The perfect combination of words will someday materialize to unlock the world's secrets, but I doubt it. Mystical means do not exist. The work is where the epiphanies lie.

In the sinister nights of my writer's soul, I remind myself how so many stories are autobiographical, and I know myself and trust my memories and powers of observation. I also have many active unfinished projects—if I am stuck on one story or poem, I switch to another. By freeing my mind and letting certain pieces rest, I attempt to solve what Wallas explains as "several problems in succession" (1926, p. 3). When I have rare moments of Illumination and understand how I might fix a narrative or verse, I "find my voice," reaching closure Welty-style in Verification—Wallas's last stage. And, yes, I base my stories on feelings—all the previous steps of Preparation, Incubation, and Illumination prepare me for the actual completion of this emotional work.

• • •

I sometimes only recognize the truth when contemplating my reflection, yet I avoid any opportunity to view myself. My physical self somehow meshes with who I am in this cloud of unknowing and self-loathing. And in my adult life, I have had far more fat mirror days than skinny mirror days. What is a fat mirror? It is a looking glass distorting me into a ghoulish funhouse attraction. Fat mirrors are perspectival, magic objects projecting wavy or grainy (or both) likenesses of the onlooker and would make even a luscious supermodel appear misshapen and disproportionate. I regard my reflection and see a Botero female with bulbous thighs and belly, puffy feet and hands.

Fat mirrors reflect the truth of aging. My haggard face.

I spot each line and bulge, but who cares about appearances? I see sadness and world-weariness in my features, observe my failures etched on my forehead and my fear of demise in the marionette lines around my mouth. Is that who I am? I can never remember feeling satisfied when I peered into a mirror at my reflection. I am an anti-Narcissus.

• • •

Julia Kristeva inspires me. I wish to tear it all down, to act "apocalyptic." While I possess a female shell, my language is on the brink of a less gender-specific focus. In "Powers of Horror" (1980/2005), Kristeva identifies a shift from feminine despair as a revolt against our mothers, those who gave us life, as we enter the male realm and discover patriarchy's unique horrors. Thus, when women experience disgust as they make themselves fit into the world of men, we simultaneously fear and *perceive* the changes we experience in perspective. Lacan's mirror reflects us in this bleak space, but these cheval glasses are funhouse props, optical illusions with no substance or endurance.

As Kristeva suggests, society prompts women to remember pre-signification when we remained helplessly attached to our mothers and absorbed what became our final destination in language systems and cognitive awareness. Nonetheless, Kristeva indicts critics' motives and the semioticians and psychoanalysts who strive to understand "abject" pre-signification and its effects on our culture. Her anger is palpable. She does not offer solutions, but recognizes how non-inclusive male theories affect individuality. She eschews amelioration by implicating and disdaining how men bury women's perspectives. However, in the end, Kristeva relents and has faith in women's abilities to overcome male power and how they might implement change: "In the meantime, let others continue their long march toward idols and truths of all kinds, buttressed with the necessarily righteous faith for wars to come, wars that will necessarily be holy" (1980/2005, p. 1139). The "I" does not matter in Kristeva's world of horrors.

I empathize deeply with any skepticism regarding society's permission for women to voice themselves. In navigating language, I am confined to words birthed in a patriarchal dominion. History scarcely records women who dared to sculpt the linguistic landscape or enrich the lexicon with their voices. Our narrative tools—diction, syntax, the very framing of reality—are forged in a male-dominated crucible. Trapped within this framework, I articulate my societal role through a language marinated in misogyny, shaped by entrenched systems from its genesis. Yet, within this paradigm, I am invisible, reduced to mere object-hood. Alienated from "culture," I linger on the periphery, fading into the backdrop the moment my object value wanes. My viewpoint is inevitably distorted—how could it not be when I must navigate the world as a woman? I attempt to understand despite my unbridled fury. My struggle and indignation are tangible.

For me, Woolf and Kristeva lay bare the consequences of male entitlement. Women define themselves in a borrowed language we can never own; we are adjuncts to the male structures that control us. And who is this Jungian "I" speaking? That "I" does not speak for me. And how far does the mirror illusion of "selfhood," our most precious possession, reach? And how can we dismantle a lie of dominant culture if it propagates and maintains a prevarication of self? Does an othering culture reflect itself over and over and over?

• • •

I can connect the creative steps outlined by Wallas and Welty to Malcolm Cowley's writing process as described in his introduction to *Writers at Work*. Cowley's ideas "click" with me (to borrow Wallas's term). To explain the composition process from an editor's perspective, Cowley describes the steps of story development:

> There would seem to be four stages in the composition of a story. First comes the germ of the story, then a period of more or less conscious meditation, then the first draft, and finally the revision, which may be simply "pencil work" …—that is, minor changes in wording—or [it] may lead to writing several drafts and what amounts to a new work. (1978, p. 10)

Indeed, generating the "germ" of a story is the most demanding phase. It feels fruitless when I go through dry periods and search for innovative ideas to express. I convince myself that all the good stories have already been told and that I am a has-been. However, each time I despair, when I am sure I will never pen another work, out of nowhere, a switch flips, and I am no longer groping for a solution or idea. Illumination! I have now come to trust that the dark moments will pass. I have learned a gardener's patience, waiting for seeds to grow, watering the black dirt, and expecting sprouts to force through the loam. But during those painful Preparation and Incubation periods that have lasted for months and years, I welcome the dim space because I trust Illumination will appear.

In the last stage, the work and toil of revision are primary; as Cowley describes it, my "several drafts" are like Welty's as she finds her voice, with the past bubbling up to inspire the present's writing decisions. One of my pieces went through over 450 significant edits, beginning at 500 words, ballooning to 80 pages, and finally deflating to about five pages. It took years, but a fine literary journal finally published my story. Though discovery is the most challenging step of creativity, my favorite part of writing and creativity is the final one after Illumination, when I can shape a crazy notion and smooth out the wrinkles. However, when I compare my process by examining Wallas's stages, insight informs each aspect of innovation. Creativity is a continuum, a Venn diagram, individual to the creator, infused with a "continuous thread of revelation."

• • •

Jewish culture has an admirable conception of mirrors. When someone dies, during a week-long period known as sitting shiva (in Hebrew, translated as "seven" for the seven days of mourning), Jewish people do not turn on any lights and cover all the mirrors in the deceased's home. During this time, no one sitting shiva peers at their reflection, and this lack of viewing underscores how humans use cheval glasses to adorn themselves and to please others. Or, by studying ourselves in a mirror, we place too much importance on our individuality, on our "I," and become selfish, losing a sense of community or feeling for others. Once someone passes away, covered mirrors enable those sitting shiva to sever any relationship of adoration and admiration with the person they have lost. And when someone passes, no one in the household must be attractive to the dead.

I long to practice shiva, cover mirrors with a dark cloth, and ignore my reflection, my hands groping at my image, gnarled and tense before me. I am a phantom pushing my way through, trusting in a shadowy world beyond my grasp. If only I could ignore reality and resurrect on the eighth day to uncover my reflection and understand who I truly am. My purpose is what I create, the relationships I forge, and the knowledge I gain. I can make my truth and develop into the person I aspire to be while writing. I aim for my negative capability; my cloudiness propels me forward.

•••

A while ago, I discovered a box of old photos in the back of my mother's closet—most of those images capture moments I have forgotten. And I found two hand-cut silhouette portraits of myself rendered years apart. My grandmother made them. What strikes me about these two silhouettes is how my face's shape and profile had not changed over many years. I distinguish all the immutable features handed down to me. Dad's brow line. Mom's cheeks. My grandmother's black eyelashes. I comprehend my creativity similarly—it is an admixture. My writing is not all my own. It is a collaboration, a layering of life's lessons. I have learned to perceive from authors of the past. When we visited museums, my mother often wrapped her Southern drawl around unfamiliar words to ask probing questions of tour guides. She was fearless. And my Grandmother Beth, the painter, pointed out a thousand shades of green in the treetops. The words I pen are a projection of what I have learned.

In seeking my voice, I often experience moments when "[s]uddenly a light is thrown back ... showing there has been a mountain of meaning rising behind you on the way you've come, is rising there still, proven now through retrospect" (Welty, 1983/2020, p. 122). As I always work to perfect my craft, my process is comparable to the steps outlined by Wallas, Welty, and Cowley. And like

Joyce and Barth's artist-protagonists, my characters often have more in common with my life experiences than I will admit. I take Welty's admonition seriously: "No art ever came out of not risking your neck" (1983/2020, p. 130). When I present my ideas, I am aiming for literary veracity. I risk my neck.

And if I am lucky enough to publish my works where I let my inner light shine, who cares if other people will recognize my glimmer or if I perceive myself positively through the fog? I must try. I must embrace my cloudiness as I attempt John Constable's clarity, who understood he could never create perfection. His paintings are radiant records of the clouds he observed two centuries ago. Perfection in imperfection.

References

Barth, J. (2006). *Lost in the funhouse: Fiction for print, tape, live voice.* Anchor Books.

Cowley, M. (1978). Introduction. In M. Cowley (Ed.), *Writers at work: The Paris review interviews* (pp. 7–22). Penguin.

Freud, S. (1995). The ego and the id. In P. Gay (Ed.), *The Freud reader* (pp. 628–658). W. W. Norton & Company. (Original work published 1923)

Hamilton, J. (2022). *John Constable: A portrait.* Pegasus Books.

Joyce, J. (1994). *A portrait of the artist as a young man.* Dover Publications.

Jung, C. G. (2005). On the concept of the archetype. In C. Harrison & P. Wood (Eds.), *Art in theory 1900–2000: An anthology of changing ideas* (2nd ed., pp. 378–381). Blackwell Publishing. (Original work published 1938)

Keats, J. (1817). Essay on poetic theory: Selections from Keats's letters. Retrieved March 23, 2024, from https://www.poetryfoundation.org/articles/69384/selections-from-keatss-letters

Kristeva, J. (2005). Powers of horror. In C. Harrison & P. Wood (Eds.), *Art in theory 1900–2000: An anthology of changing ideas* (2nd ed., pp. 1137–1139). Blackwell Publishing. (Original work published 1980)

Lacan, J. (2005). The mirror-phase. In C. Harrison & P. Wood (Eds.), *Art in theory 1900–2000: An anthology of changing ideas* (2nd ed., pp. 620–624). Blackwell Publishing. (Original work published 1949)

Leslie, R. C. (1896). *Life and letters of John Constable, R. A.* Chapman and Hall.

Poincaré, H. (2019). *The foundations of science: Science and hypothesis, the value of science, science, and method.* Good Press. (Original work published 1904)

Wallas, G. (1926). *The art of thought.* Harcourt, Brace and Company.

Welty, E. (2020). *One writer's beginnings.* Scribner. (Original work published 1983)

Woolf, V. (2002). *A room of one's own* [E-book]. Project Gutenberg of Australia. (Original work published 1929)

PART 2

Construction

∵

To tell a story is to reconstruct the conditions of reality in order to manipulate or change them.

RACHEL CUSK, "'The Art of Fiction No. 246,' *Paris Review*"

••

CHAPTER 10

Primary Sources

My Fiction as Creative Dialectic

1   Crafting Truths

In this book's essays, I have already explained why I write and my authorial processes. However, to write well, I must engage deeply with literary works that influence my approach. This analysis involves a two-pronged process: detailed close readings comparing my own to the works that inspire me to follow cursory literature reviews of influential texts.

In exploring literary scholarship, my inquiries are not straightforward. I often ask myself, *How can my composition of short fiction enable me to craft "truthful" stories?* When I ask this question, I also investigate how short fiction might express the innermost truths and circumstances that constrain other women's autonomy. My queries help me understand the intersection of narrative forms, truth, and gender dynamics in fiction. My approaches and scholarly work apply a multi-faceted methodological approach tailored to unravel such complex ideas. This work acknowledges my unique position as an academic straddling the practices of creative writing and scholarly analysis. A commitment to engagement is integral to my research.

First, I use rigorous textual analysis, examining works of short fiction through a theoretical lens, specifically a feminist perspective. This scrutiny is not a mere exploration of texts, but an immersive inquiry into how sociocultural and historical contexts shape narrative forms and themes. Second, I embrace hybridized research, a practice where writing is a creative means to an end and a tool for inquiry and reflection. This approach grants me an experiential understanding of the challenges and revelations I encounter when I write "truthfully" about women's lives and experiences. The scare quotes here acknowledge the irony of writing truthful fiction, a topic I tackle in the first section of this book. Textual analysis combined with practice-based research offers a comprehensive understanding of how short fiction reflects and deconstructs the complex truths of women's attempts at autonomy. My creative practices and scholarly analyses converge in this hybrid space of feminism.

The following cursory critique of literature is a mere snippet of my research. I have limited my analysis to specific texts, which empower me to situate my creativity on the canon's continuum. I also stake claims for women's literature,

© CATE MCGOWAN, 2025 | DOI:10.1163/9789004712379_010

where my ideas might contribute new insights. Brief close readings of my texts complementing literature analyses of canonical works will reveal more than anything I might say about my creative output. I focus on authorial choices, narrative structure, and thematic elements, particularly as they relate to the representation of women's experiences and autonomy. Through close readings, I uncover layers of meaning and technique in the texts and how the works guide me. Thus, my research bridges the gap between the theoretical perspectives and the specificities of discrete texts, providing a superficial understanding of the literary landscape surrounding the women's short fiction I explicate.

· · ·

My love of reading brought me to writing. I could not put down certain books on sunny days as a kid, even when outdoor playtime beckoned. When Beth died in *Little Women*, I cried; I cheered Pippi's slapstick antics in *Pippi Longstocking*. Those childhood books inspired my curiosity; while reading, I was living someone's important story. Now I know this phenomenon is "[the] willing suspension of disbelief," as the poet Samuel Taylor Coleridge famously articulates (1834/2021, p. 1). Authors use this method to create reality in their stories.

For authors to create works that might assist the reader in suspending disbelief, they must find new ways of seeing the world—looking at it with childlike curiosity is what I do when I write to elicit wonder. In my work, I hope to reveal feminine experiences and capture how humans constantly battle emotional tension below the surface of their seemingly ordinary lives. Depicting the imperceptible dimensions of emotion in my fiction is crucial. While modern concepts ground my writing and theoretical framework, I often visit a veritable "Hall of Ancestors," the philosophers and theorists who laid the foundation for the theories of Tzvetan Todorov and Mieke Bal.

Some of these older theories help me understand Coleridge's suspension of disbelief: 18th-century philosophers Edmund Burke (1759/1958) and Immanuel Kant (1790/1951) presented theories of the sublime to explain how we experience awe or terror in the face of something vast and unknown. This feeling of the sublime even occurs when we are reading. I have often felt the sublime as I delved into a great novel and have wanted to mimic this effect. Both Burke and Kant believe the sublime is a form of heightened awareness that takes us beyond the limits of our understanding and leads us to contemplate something approaching divinity or, at the very least, what is an infinite and superior understanding. Sigmund Freud's theory of the uncanny from his essay of the same name, "The Uncanny" (1919/2003), further explains the experience of encounters that seem both familiar and alien at the same time, uncomfortable and, therefore, uncanny.

These concepts are particularly relevant when considering Coleridge's "suspension of disbelief"; a reader experiences an immersive, novel feeling, yet the story seems strangely familiar. Both Burke and Kant's theories of the sublime and Freud's ideas about the uncanny work to create that sense of wonderment that Coleridge is speaking about, articulating a sense of losing oneself in a story, of the feeling when a reader is so transfixed, they forget for a few moments who and what they are.

As a reader and writer, my challenge is sustaining wonder in the Coleridgean sense. I want to be immersed in a story when I read, and I want my readers to experience the same: the opportunity to escape from their everyday routines and to think about something new, an idea that will change how they interact with others or events. To build a believable universe where I can suspend readers' disbelief, I need to slowly bring readers into the story's world, allowing them to notice details as they begin to understand the setting and context. As a result, readers will start to gain a new comprehension of the fabricated world in which the story plays out. And perhaps, they will look at their own lives differently.

As I study a limited selection of fiction written by women in this book, I have begun to understand why some literature is unputdownable. To be a writer, I must be a reader first. I must study the works that create intense immersion. As a writer, I must strenuously parse the texts I admire to understand how they work; I must look under the hood and identify the parts of the engine that drive a story. I actively work on tinkering with my craft through intensive reading. My tune-ups review philosophy and the ideas underpinning literature. Writing is the drag race to the finish line.

• • •

Unlike Freud's exploration of the uncanny, Tzvetan Todorov's 1970 study, *Introduction a la littérature fantastique* (it appeared in English in 1975 as *The Fantastic: A Structural Approach to a Literary Genre*), attempts to analyze literature using literary tropes. Todorov's ideas were the first narratological approach to tackle the concept of "the fantastic" and remain a starting point in examining less realistic fictional depictions. Todorov's theory of the fantastic is controversial, as critics regard it as a standard for literary analysis or pan it for being too limited a paradigm. Indeed, every theoretical approach to fantastic narratives incorporates or refutes Todorov's concepts. According to Todorov, the foremost characteristic of the fantastic is an element of "hesitation," in which both reader and characters are uncertain whether unusual events in a narrative disrupt the recognizable or "real" world and confuse interpretation. The reader might vacillate between reason or attributing the unexplainable in a story to supernatural causes (Todorov, 1975, pp. 25–27).

Todorov insists that fantastic narratives cannot be read as "allegorical" or "poetic" in nature (Todorov, 1975, pp. 24–40). He argues that once a text has a second meaning, the literal sense (in which the supernatural has been suggested) loses its hold on the reader (Todorov, 1975, p. 33). Therefore, the fantastic is distinguished from "marvelous" literature and the "uncanny." In uncanny or strange literature, the unusual or bizarre elements in the narrative are resolved when the narrator, or other circumstances, offer us a rational explanation for what has occurred, thereby eliminating any hesitation or ambiguity characteristic of what was fantastic. In fantastic literature, conversely, the element of doubt for the reasons behind occurrences never plays a part in the account. Instead, the fantastic, which includes fairy tales, myths, folklore, and fables, does not pretend to reproduce a world inhabited by facsimiles of regular persons (Todorov, 1975, pp. 41–56). By reading the phrase, *they lived happily ever after*, or other familiar semantic cues, such as *once upon a time*, readers agree with authors to abandon all notions of verisimilitude, consequently immersing themselves entirely in an alternative world unlike their own.

Alternatively, fantastic narratives situate stories in familiar worlds; therefore, any unexplainable circumstance disrupts those environments, creating a crisis for characters and readers. However, Todorov's strict, structuralist approach to story parsing is potentially a problematic lens for interpretation because it stresses that the fantastic cannot truly be defined. Because Todorov denies any possibility of allegorical readings, his theory dooms the fantastic to literal readings and feeds the widespread conception that fantastic literature is escapist.

I have narrowed my analysis of Todorov to focus on the elements of his ideas that I find helpful. Most of these concepts align with my understanding of Narratology, a structuralist theory in its diverse approaches to narrative. Narratological theories create a base for my views about storytelling, examining how disparate tales compare and color perceptions of the world. The multifarious theses attempt to understand how stories differ from other rhetoric and prose. Narrative forms give people vital information and ways to communicate and convey their perceptions of space, time, and human circumstances. Stories also allow people to assign meaning to their experiences. Much of my work derives from this understanding of how narratives are a primary method of conveying information. Analyzing my work through a narratology lens, I might understand my intentions.

Narratology includes studying the chronology of events, actions, and scenes and how characters and settings determine the arc of a narrative. Stories create context with settings using milieus, not only locations or temporal conditions. Finally, a narratological study examines how a story is told, including the narrative's perspective. Narratology is this method of studying a story's form.

Mieke Bal identifies Narratology's emotional consequences for humans' self-understanding in her earnest, pointed exploration in *Narratology: Introduction to the Theory of Narrative*, which appeared in 1985; under the aegis of Structuralism, she provides a comprehensive introduction to theories of narrative texts. Bal distills how we understand "literary and non-literary works" (1985/2009, p. 1). This theory studies how narratives work and how their inherent forms influence their reception. The book comprises three sections: "Text: Words," focusing on how to discuss the layers in texts; "Story: Aspects," focusing on the connective components of a narrative; and "Fabula: Elements," looking at how chronology works in stories. I am particularly interested in Fabula:

> [T]he fabulas of most narrative texts do display some form of homology, both with a sentence structure and with "real-life." Consequently, most fabulas can be said to be constructed according to the demands of human "logic of events," provided that this concept is not too narrowly understood. (Bal, 1985/2009, p. 184)

Thus, Bal explores Fabula's chronological factors and stories' dependence on contrary, realistic elements. This inclusive, dualistic critique informs my creative work's attempts to translate my experiences onto the page.

• • •

As another way to examine texts, Reader-Response Theory explores the relationship between readers' feelings and the literature they read. Reader-Response theory (Transactional Theory) emerged in the mid-20th century, championed by figures such as Louise Rosenblatt, Stanley Fish, and Wolfgang Iser. This movement sought to shift the focus of literary criticism from analyzing texts to emphasizing the reader's roles as vital contributors in interpretive processes—a symbiosis. Reader-Response theorists approach literature with a unique kind of authorial humility, treating the text as an invitation to an audience's imagination, not an escapist fantasy that exists outside of the readers' lived experiences. Reading becomes a contract for the reader and the text, a relationship evoking an occasion or meaning for the individual reader. In Rosenblatt's essay, "Transaction Versus Interaction: A Terminology Rescue Operation" (1985), Reader-Response encourages an open-mindedness foundational to a democratic society.

Reader-Response theorists are interested in the "how" of interpreting a text; they are primarily unconcerned with the "what." Instead, they focus on the possible "when," "whom," and "why" in the interpretation process. A central tenet of the theory is the reader's role in fashioning their own narrative of the work from the one the author provides. A text is a collection of signs that stand for something more significant: a series of "chunks" of information. The reader responds to the information in the text and works to "read" or interact with it. The reader's narrative reveals infinite possibilities for interpretation and acceptance.

E. D. Hirsch, Jr.'s (2006) controversial, neoconservative hermeneutics of reading, one of encoding/decoding, requires readers to interpret texts actively by activating their world experience. This theory applies to sound, image, emotion, and language. Once readers have decoded a text, they may find new meaning in their experiences. Encoding and decoding concepts provides readers with valuable insights; however, I find Hirsch's politics and those he has inspired problematic. Similarly, Reader-Response theorists argue that no matter what else a narrative is about, it will evoke emotions in the reader. In short, universal emotions arising from our experiences make original stories possible. A narrative is an interaction; without interaction, the reader cannot respond emotionally.

For Reader-Response Theory to emphasize the reader's part in meaning-making, a complete text is created between the reader's reaction and the construal of what they have read instead of the narrative functioning as an assemblage. With this whole, the reader constructs meaning and and their own interpretations of a text, which is an emotional response. Additionally, Reader-Response Theory pursues both content and context. However, it is not concerned with the specific content of the text itself; it invests in the overall theme of the narrative and how it fits the larger context of the author's creation.

Since the 1980s, Postcritique has questioned trends in literary studies and the certainty of interpretive methods, noting how criticism has become overly theoretical. In the subsequent decades, many scholars, including Rita Felski, have elaborated on what they conceive as the shortcomings of over-analysis. While some critics view Postcritique as simply an aestheticization of critique, others have found it to provide supplemental analyses and new interpretative practices.

Moving beyond a reader's role in criticism, Postcritique attempts to find new methods of interpreting and digesting literature's past established forms, enabling literary theory to move in new directions. From the 1960s through the 1980s, Hans-Georg Gadamer (1984) and Paul Ricœur (2008) strongly associated with a hermeneutics of suspicion, a mode of reading believed to be characteristic of the self-referential of the postmodern. Around the same time, Jacques Derrida posited his unstable signifiers of Deconstructionism, which he first examined in the late 1970s and published in English in *Positions* (1981). Ricœur initially conceptualized Postcritique in *Freud and Philosophy: An Essay on Interpretation* (1965); he was inspired by how Freud, Marx, and Nietzsche posit texts might often present misleading or overly simplistic surfaces. Beneath these texts' smooth veneers, they conceal complex, underlying significances. In his book, Ricœur contends that because appearances are deceptive, texts contain more profound content implications.

In *After Critique*, Mitchum Huehls argues that "the problem" with critique is that it has become a "default" interpretive lens, a crutch (2016, p. 182). He calls for a "Postcritique" sensibility in which we use critique as merely one set of tools among others when engaging with texts (Huehls, 2016, p. XII). Huehls' analogy for this hermeneutics of suspiciously listening—in which we ask questions like, "What is elided here?" and "What is assumed here?"—comes from literary studies where the deconstruction has made critique a singular focus among scholars (2016, p. 151).

As Postcritique proves, there are other ways of reading (and writing). However, criticism has its limits. In *After Theory*, Terry Eagleton discusses the bounds of critique, "the taxing business of trying to grasp what is actually going on" (2004, p. 223). This attempt to interpret what we read demands that we prioritize what we know about reality before making sense of literary texts. Indeed, considering context and perspective is also essential. Different people from disparate backgrounds experience reality differently.

Rita Felski views Postcritique as a reaction to criticism's overuse. Postcritique is not against critique, but as she claims in *The Uses of Literature*, diverse kinds of readings are relevant: "[T]here is no reason why our readings cannot blend analysis and attachment, criticism and love" (2008, p. 22). Felski, in a later book, *The Limits of Critique* (2015), clarifies that she is not hostile to criticism (2015, p. 5). Similarly, critique is valuable but insufficient for comprehending the depth and breadth of literature; other interpretative practices should supplement it. Felski focuses on reparative literature as a more viable route. Felski and critic Elizabeth S. Anker contend in their 2017 book *Critique and Postcritique* that interrogations of texts are disputable (2017, p. 1). Counter to valuing close reading's ability to reveal hidden meanings in the text, the ambition of reparative reading is to reevaluate reading by acknowledging the worth and consequence of amateur criticism by so-called "bad readers."

Many proponents of Postcritique also theorize that employing the interpretative techniques associated with meticulous textual analysis might produce inconclusive or mundane conclusions. Some critics have even called for a revolution of the ordinary or even unlearning academic reading habits. A postcritical reading of literary texts instead highlights the reader's sensibility and uncovers echoes of subconscious states spurred by the contents of a particular text. It might also focus on a specific traditional motif or discuss feelings of uneasiness or anguish dredged up by the text.

By exploring my relationships with stories and how I critique the works of others and my own, I aim to provide a thorough and innovative analysis that shows how narratives have the potential to catalyze reader empathy. Examining the theoretical bases of prose and poetry and applying the theoretical concepts to literary works helps me to compose.

• • •

My primary purpose as a critic is to understand women's perspectives, and I read literature through a feminist filter fitted over other lenses of theories and literary genres. All the different approaches I have learned and used culminate in my focus on feminist literary theories.

Since women began fighting for equal rights in modern society and through all five waves of feminism, the feminist struggle and resistance have manifested in different forms, including liberal, Marxist, postmodernist, and radical feminism. With its post-structuralist inclusiveness, feminist literary theory (FLT) challenges religious and mythological ideas of women. It indicts the past's objectifying texts representing female or female-identifying characters as a subjugated class. Feminist close reading is thus inherently Marxist. But the crux of FLT argues there is no fixed "female voice" and that contends women should produce their symbols and language to express themselves exclusively.

Fiction by women allows them to imagine a world in ways they may not experience in real life. Hélène Cixous' influential essay, "The Laugh of the Medusa," also promotes the idea that women should "write themselves" and explore innovative ways to create and analyze women's writing. Initially published in 1975 in French as *"Le Rire de la Méduse,"* Cixous's work provides an insightful evaluation of patriarchy, explicating feminist ideals grounded with post-structuralist and psychoanalytic theories, proposing a fundamental change with *écriture féminine* ("feminine writing"): "Woman must write her self. ... Woman must put herself into the text—as into the world and into history—by her own movement" (1976, p. 875).

And Cixous's view of women's erasure, "white ink" (1976, p. 881), bolsters the concept promoting "writing of oneself," erstwhile writing invisible on a white page. This white ink indicates places and spaces not yet written into a text but assumed in existence as opposed to men's authoritative black print. Indeed, "Laugh" is a call to action, an appeal to women to enact their desires and gain agency by writing about their experiences.

Over the past century, women writers have written exemplary works confronting social limitations. Many of these female authors seethe, creating conditions so abhorrent for their female characters that it is apparent the authors' principal aim is to expose society's deplorable treatment of women. Locating an author within their literary era and writing milieu helps contextualize their work (leading to a comparison with male writerly examples of corresponding times), there are fewer distinct literary epochs for women than men. Female work does not belong to any specific era, but transcends the time of its creation. Women's work exists on a continuum.

Because I read women's short stories as closely as I study scholarship analyzing the texts' functions, feminist transgressive works inform my reading and critical practice because they question women's subordinate social standing. I study these sources (works of poetry, fiction, and scholarship) to locate how each piece deploys elements of fiction that might expose women's secondary status. Other feminist critics precede me. Rosalind Coward, in her 1980 essay, "'This Novel Changes Lives': Are Women's Novels Feminist Novels? A Response to Rebecca O'Rourke's Article 'Summer Reading,'" asks if women's novels must be feminist and questions the very elements necessary for a feminist classification.

Also, I break down the works I study and admire, aiming to prove how the disparate styles of Gertrude Stein, Virginia Woolf, María Luisa Bombal, and Leonora Carrington are feminist at their core. In 1996, another feminist critic, Mary Eagleton, muses in *Working with Feminist Criticism* if there is pleasure in women remaining silent when speaking out against oppression and if keeping secrets is preferable for a peaceful existence. This stance is concerning, embracing the silence of women and the "go along to get along" conviction many women have enacted to survive. Shirley Jackson's explorations of women's unfulfilling quotidian lives might obliquely prove Eagleton's suppositions, but Jackson also underscores what happens when women cannot speak freely.

Other critics, Sandra Gilbert and Susan Gubar, in their work from the late 1970s, *The Madwoman in the Attic: The Woman Writer and the Nineteenth-Century Literary Imagination,* consider if intentional feminist close-readings originate with the writer or reader. Elaine Showalter engages Gilbert and Gubar in her 2011 book, *Gilbert and Gubar's* The Madwoman in the Attic *after Thirty Years*, to explore why so many mentally disordered women inhabit literature. The fiction of Angela Carter, Lorrie Moore, and Kelly Link might respond to the women's problems that feminist critics also lay bare. These three authors feature homemakers and average women coping with the rage and murderous urges lurking under their placid façades. In her aptly titled "Visual Pleasure and Narrative Cinema" (1975), Laura Mulvey, art historian and film theorist, notes society's continued objectification of women and how aesthetics connect visual pleasure with the male gaze. Similarly, Angela Carter's florid and visually descriptive prose shows how centralized the male gaze is in our culture and how it might affect women's behavior as they try to survive in patriarchal systems. María Luisa Bombal, decades before Mulvey, also explores the placement of a matriarch serving a dual role as a decorative fixture *and* protagonist in *The Shrouded Woman*.

• • •

How did I get here? My literary and critical interests have pushed me to combine my efforts. What I read and how I read directly inform my compositions, so this literature review chapter scrutinizes the influences shaping my writing output. In my junior year in college, I met a good friend for dinner at a café. Her family came along. As we dug into our appetizers, Dana explained to her father how we had met in a critical theory class. He was unimpressed. The good man, a poet and professor at a different university, knew his way around criticism. But he did not like it. He raised his hands to the ceiling and yelled defiantly above the restaurant's din, "No mo po-mo, you boho mofos!" (Translation: "No more Postmodernism, you Bohemian m*therf*ckers").

After the professor calmed down, he made a valid point (this time in a stage whisper): "This stupid new *criticism* [emphasis on the word "criticism"] doesn't leave room for art or beauty. It's all about the construct ... the *signs*." The man's disgust confused me because I loved parsing signs—my undergraduate classes in comparative literature were so immersive and thought-provoking that I had never considered the topics I was studying were unorthodox or revolutionary. They were staid orthodoxy to me. My studies were meaningful until those same theories came to loggerheads with my creative and artistic ambitions. I have struggled to reconcile my interest in hermeneutics and my passion for creative writing.

Criticism *and* art exploration provide me with a quarry of self-discovery. Whether I am poring over an analysis of context or composing a surrealist scene for a short story, I consider myself a literary "digger." In my critical and creative endeavors, I burrow deep into untilled territory to unearth innovative ideas. I explore these terrains not to innovate, but to fertilize my fiction as I search for the best ways to interpret and further the feminist literary canon. My cartographical work in criticism provides the longitudinal and latitudinal limits for my creative work's landscapes. In my short stories, I explore the fragility of life, coupling characters who seek agency with quirky settings departing from realistic depictions.

It is crucial to acknowledge that beginning a survey with my chosen writers is a convenient starting point, but it is not the beginning of women authors' essential contributions. Society only encouraged most women to read and write in the last century, and communities in many corners of our planet still do not educate women in 2024, let alone exalt female accomplishments. Also, beginning my literature survey in the early twentieth century privileges a Western male point of view, and male privilege has stayed the same. Of course, if an argument focuses on current hegemonic power structures, one must also confront the problems of colonial and neo-colonial rule; however, a particular focus on these essential theories is impossible in such a limited contextualization as this one, especially when I already have so many threads to pull.

••

I categorize works. I do not mean to do it. Compartmentalization is a side effect of many literary theories' rigid adherence to specific reading methods. Nonetheless, in formal and traditional interpretations of literature, the process of close reading, a practice eschewed in some contemporary criticism circles, is unquestionably relevant when analyzing works whose subject tackles the very process of writing. Thus, we must at least acknowledge the role of authorship (the author is not always dead). If we do not, we lose sight of why a piece was written in the first place. Indeed, books often exemplify the social difficulties and changes that disrupted the authors' worlds.

I examine short fiction works produced by women in this book. Though I am interested in other representations of alterity, it is impractical to include all the influences informing my stories—a study of that magnitude would constitute an encyclopedia. Of course, not all men write to relegate women to second-sex status, but in our society, gender holds sway in privileging men's compositions over women's writing. I am not inclined to reinforce a paradigm centralizing Western male points of view and articulation for constructing feminine authorial identity, so I begin my review with Gertrude Stein and Virginia Woolf's modernist perspectives.

Most importantly, my quest for emotional truth defines my practice-based research as an author. In my reading practice, I choose not to favor genres or gender-specific writers; however, I have chosen only women's fiction to examine as primary sources. Specifically, I examine how the high modernist works of Gertrude Stein's *Tender Buttons* and Virginia Woolf's *Orlando* reveal female authors trying to "rewrite" literary norms and realities for women. As a departure from the fractured realities of Modernism's nonlinear plots and Postmodernism's meta-characterizations, the magical realist work of María Luisa Bombal and the surreal stories of Leonora Carrington allow for imagining alternative worlds where female characters might possess complete agency or encounter bigotry as something altogether different from patriarchal misogyny. Building on these earlier women authors' sense of the uncanny and fantastic,

I explore Angela Carter's contemporary retellings of contemporary fairytales, and I focus on Shirley Jackson and Lorrie Moore's slant representations of women's everyday lives. Finally, in Kelly Link's work, supernatural elements expose deeply flawed protagonists and mystical forces claiming authority over humans. In all my examinations, I critique how literary forms might transgress society's status quo for people.

• • •

My reading critiques inspire my stories. At its core, my fiction is practice-based research focusing on feminist messages, but most importantly, my work echoes my experiences. But how can I affect change as a fiction writer? Is this possible? Sociologist Patricia Leavy's qualitative work, as presented in "Fiction, Feminism, and Qualitative Research: An Interview with Dr. Patricia Leavy" (2019), discusses the activism of arts-based research, explaining how qualitative research might effectively use fiction to illustrate difficult-to-convey information. But she also discusses how fiction can disclose truths other forms of writing cannot:

> As a writer, there's so much you can do with fiction that you can't do with nonfiction. One of the advantages of fiction is that an author can portray interiority. This reflex to explore the deep waters of the psyche offers scholars enormous potential to make micro-macro links by showing what people do versus what they think and feel. Fiction allows us to show the gap. Fiction also allows us to portray people's vulnerabilities in compelling ways, and those are the things that connect us to each other. It's also about how we can reach people through fiction. It's about how readers approach and process fiction. For starters, most people see reading fiction as a pleasurable, leisure time activity. People's defenses are dialed down. That's a quite different frame of mind than when one is reading academic nonfiction or hearing a lecture. Fiction also promotes empathetic engagement and compassion. (Leavy, 2019, p. 2929)

Certainly, my examinations of primary works of women's literature prioritize how fiction invites readers to observe characters' interior lives. Fiction offers the reader specific perspectives best revealed through experience rather than data or theory, a phenomenological or pseudo-ethnographic focus.

When I initially embarked on my latest writing adventure, I found I had composed and compiled over a hundred pages of stories. I tip my hat to the work influencing me. The current draft of my story collection, *Cherry Bomb*, was born out of an accumulated awareness and appreciation of narrative theories and periods of literature. While I focus on secondary sources and criticism in my contextualization, I am also concerned with how I might convey genuine feelings through fictional representations. My short stories closely consider how life and reality are alterable. Emotional truth is malleable and relative to my fictional characters. How might shifting moralities and ambitions affect people? I address this question of deeper sub-themes within my tales.

Through a practice-based close-up lens in *Cherry Bomb*, I focus on the psychic pain women might experience in their life stages as they forge ahead in a hostile world and face adversity. My collection of tales tackles how people, especially females, battle real and imagined enemies, metaphysical and psychological. As my plural first-person narrator in "Reservoir" tells the reader, "The triumphant monster carries us far away into a deep ocean where the fish don't have eyes" (McGowan, 2019e, para. 2). Indeed, every person clashes with monsters in their imagination.

Practice-based research suits my purposes. I use my creative writing to make scholarly discoveries, insights, and observations. Further, my research differs from composing stories; instead, I supply original approaches and techniques beyond what an individual artist might contribute to scholarship via structured processes. As I have learned outside academia, practice-based products reach beyond scholarly contexts.

• • •

The stories in my latest collection study and uncover how a woman's interactions affect her identity. I de-internalize the micro- and macro-aggressions I have absorbed over the years, how a male-centered society demands women fulfill roles and duties as mothers, homemakers, friends, and sexual companions. My stories' autobiographical details allow me to present a different type of personal truth when I create fictional females who experience the same limitations I encounter.

As a researcher, I delve into autoethnography and autofiction, methodologies intertwining the personal with the academic. These approaches are integral to my exploration of women's autonomy and truth. Autoethnography is a means of incorporating my firsthand experiences into my creative works. The term is a portmanteau combining "autobiography" and "ethnography," a compound of two forms of rhetorical composition. However, autoethnography is not primarily literary in function; instead, it is a mode of academic inquiry in which a scholar researches a topic of personal significance (for example, a family immigration story), positioning their experiences within a social context and through their unique perspective.

Autoethnography requires a researcher's introspection about their social position, feelings, and knowledge as they apply these personal perspectives to a social condition under examination. As Elizabeth Ettorre explains in *Autoethnography as Feminist Method: Sensitising the Feminist "I"* (2017), autoethnographic writing "allow[s] interpretations of personal 'truths' and speak[s] about oneself to transform into narrative representations" of research (p. 3). By examining how I have internalized society's messages, echoing Ettorre's definition of autoethnography, my fiction is an essential expression of myself.

Arthur P. Bochner, in "On First-Person Narrative Scholarship: Autoethnography as Acts of Meaning" (2012), notes how autoethnography allows scholars to elect narrative exposition to present their research and through giving access to their inner lives:

> The functions of stories and storytelling in creating and managing identity; the expressive forms for making sense of lived experience and communicating it to others; the entanglements that permeate how interpersonal life is lived and how it is told to others; the reflexive dimensions of the relationships between storytellers and story listeners; and the canonical narratives that circulate through society, offering scripted ways of acting. (pp. 155–156)

As told through stories, an author's elucidations of accumulated knowledge might be a valid research method for interpreting complex humanistic inquiry. Through the pages of my story, "The Last Days of Men," the narrator echoes my feelings and experiences:

> I'd never known luck or possessed uncanny skills. Nothing ever came easy for me. I did not understand what having perfect pitch or a green thumb meant. I'd never pulled a one-armed bandit and lined up three bells. (McGowan, 2020a, para. 37)

My story reveals my truth masked as fiction presented as a narrator's struggle.

Bochner explains storytelling is a different truth: "[T]hey're emotional, dialogic, and collaborative truths. ... [T]hus I am not so much aiming for some goal called 'Truth' as for an enlarged capacity to deal with life's challenges and contingencies" (2012, p. 161). Truth is the core concept I endeavor to expose in my fiction, but "true" truth is what I am writing. Autoethnography is not precisely what I am doing.

Autoethnography uses my experiences as a primary data source and molds them into meaningful prose for others. Through my reflective process, I reflect upon my journey as a female writer and scholar and how these identities intersect and influence my understanding. Autoethnography goes beyond mere personal narrative; it is a tool for examining broader cultural phenomena through the lenses of my individual experiences. When I weave theoretical analyses into my narratives, I can provide a deeper understanding of my topics, especially those related to gender, identity, and autonomy.

Autofiction, the creative counterpart of autoethnography, blends autobiography and fiction. In my autofictional writing, I create stories from my unique life events. This method allows me to explore the themes of my focus—such as the constraints and expressions of women's autonomy—in a personally authentic and creatively expansive manner. Autofiction is a conduit through which I can investigate and express the nuanced realities of women's lives, blending the factual and fictional to capture deeper truths. I can present my unique perspective because I use autoethnography and autofiction in my research, approaching subjects from a place of personal authenticity while also exploring fanciful ideas.

Why does it sound boring when someone tries to recount a dream they had the night before? Words fail to describe the surreality, atmospheres, and emotions I encounter on unusual journeys in REM land. The same goes for writing fiction. How might I draw on my own experiences to create exciting tales? I am writing autofiction. This mash-up of "autobiography" and "fiction," a portmanteau like autoethnography's "autobiography" and "ethnography," suits me perfectly; it is an oxymoronic concept labeling fictional literature autobiographical, a fictional account in nature or, because of its inspiration, true prevarication. In describing his 1977 book, *Fils*, on the back cover, Serge Doubrovsky explains that aspects of his novel are autofiction. Doubrovsky explains that most *"fiction d'évènements et de faits strictement réels"* ("fiction about completely real events and facts"), like its cousin literary form the *roman-à-clef*, is written by commonplace persons, not by the *"importants de ce monde"* ("important people in the world") (1977). A narrator and author can be the same person. The form is not only postmodernist, but quotidian.

However, most fiction writers will argue that their stories are already autobiographical, as they draw on their firsthand experiences and observations when writing. "Write what you know." In introducing *The Story of "Me": Contemporary American Autofiction* (2018), Marjorie Worthington attempts to explain autofiction. She notes:

> Doubrovsky's definition of autofiction dictates that it must not stray too far from the accurate representation of extratextual events. In possible contradiction of that mandate, Doubrovsky publishes his texts under the rubric of *novel*, a term traditionally used to refer to fictional narratives. His insistence that autofiction tell a referential story belies the label of novel. (Worthington, 2018, p. 13)

In my latest story collection, *Cherry Bomb*, I reveal my life experiences through my fiction and explore ways women might resist patriarchal systems that privilege masculinity and hetero-normativity. I tell stories that reveal transcendence in rare moments, but include lighthearted moments to ease the pain of characters experiencing separation, the fear of failure, and the fear of not being loved.

These are my origin stories, transformative work as mandated by autoethnography standards, but they are more. They are autofiction.

2   Close Readings

2.1   *Gertrude Stein*

As I study literary movements from the past hundred years, the authors who interest me are the ones who have shifted expectations and explored new ways of telling stories; they are those who defy easy classification. Gertrude Stein reconfigures culture and modernizes theories. Stein's 1914 collection of axiomatic nomenclature, *Tender Buttons: Objects, Food, Rooms*, blurs the borders between poetry and fiction in which each entry defiantly reconstitutes meaning. In *Tender Buttons*, Stein accomplishes the hybridity I aim to imitate. Stein replaces poetic end-stopped lines as she redefines words based on their etymology, plays with sounds and syllables, chooses terms for their impact and playfulness, and juxtaposes them to overthrow common significations.

The male gaze cannot survive Stein's eye. Each snippet toys with audible effects. She begins with "A Carafe, That Is a Blind Glass" (Stein, 1914/2012, p. 1), presenting an impractical object not commonly found in feminine domestic spaces, though it sports a voluptuous shape. Additionally, Stein refers to dresses, earrings, and purses, all feminine adornments reconfiguring patriarchal language with male descriptions and objects feminized. Stein mentions the female names "Pauline" (1914/2012, p. 13) and "Mildred" (p. 4), referring to "ladies" and "sisters" throughout. As a postmodernist, John Barth equates authorship with omnipotence in his story collection *Lost in the Funhouse: Fiction for Print, Tape, Live Voice;* Stein's work predicts this concept, featuring a god-like reconfiguration of material reality 65 years before the fiction of Barth appeared.

2.1.1   "Unrhymed Sonnet": A Response to Stein

In *Tender Buttons*, Stein exploits how form might enhance content. She uses the dictionary or guidebook structure as a steady base for her wild semiotic experiments. Some of my attempts at prose poetry and micro-fiction experiment with form similarly—for example, my hermit-crab story "Unrhymed Sonnet Constructed with American Sentences" (McGowan, 2020d). What exactly is a hermit-crab story? A hermit crab protects its tender abdomen with scavenged shells and objects, and writers who use the hermit-crab form, as Brenda Miller explains in her essay, "The Shared Space Between Reader and Writer: A Case Study" (2015), write narratives appropriating other forms—emails, recipes, to-do lists, field guides, obituaries, Q&A, crossword puzzles, to name a few.

In her 2018 pedagogical essay "Using Poetic Forms in Nonfiction," poet and essayist Heidi Czerwiec discusses the hermit-crab method and how verse forms act as "scaffolds" for prose and are helpful for unfettering content and reinforcing themes (para. 3). I try to do the same in my narratives. Sure, "Unrhymed Sonnet" is fourteen lines, so visually, it is a poem with stanzas—an octave and sestet, a Petrarchan sonnet:

> After you turned ten, you tossed then lost pink clackers on low power lines.
> That spring, rain-swelled creeks rose, an angry orange raging across your yard.
> The woods brimmed like a sink basin, and your red playhouse slid off its blocks.
> You pedaled home in another May cloudburst, scudded the muddy slopes.
> Your soaked Schwinn's brakes failed steering the steep driveway, and you hit the brick house.
> Gears gone, wheels crimped, jaw cracked, chin gashed, you staggered, dragged a blood trail inside.
> The E.R. visit drained the family's savings, and your mom blamed you. As usual, not the black clouds: Girl, you've stirred trouble for the last time.
>
> Still not blessed, you plan to meet your divorce lawyer at the library.
> You slow current through stacks where homeless men hide from summer—it's fucking hot.
> Moisture from June humidity slinks in, loosens the glue on books' spines.
> You think about making plans, but carrying an umbrella's pointless.
> In Periodicals, you sweat tabloids about royal weddings.
> Before your attorney arrives. You bail, blame yourself, the storms you've got. (McGowan, 2020d)

This piece is not accentual and does not rhyme, so it is not a sonnet. Or is it?

Nonetheless, its long lines *are* syllabic, using American sentences, a form introduced by Beat poet Allen Ginsberg comprising seventeen syllables—the same amount as haiku (1999, p. 79). My technical restrictions for this poem echo Stein's constraints on her aphoristic re-definitions. "Unrhymed Sonnet" is a short hybrid story exploring a woman's disappointments as a child and adult, repeating the motifs of childhood play and activities in other tales in my collection, "Reservoir" (McGowan, 2019e) and "Depending on the Horizon" (McGowan, 2018a). The water allusions stream through the descriptions and action verbs. Additional narratives in my compilation work to expose parental and romantic disenchantment, "Unrhymed Sonnet" addresses accountability with its second-person speaker/narrator.

2.2 *Virginia Woolf*

Virginia Woolf's *Orlando: A Biography*, published in 1928, predicts the postmodernist foci of emotional ambivalence, mood swings, and malleable personalities presented in twentieth-century modernist works. However, the themes found in *Orlando*, including lost innocence, late blossoming, and recycled language, are also postmodernist; a strict dividing line between Modernism and Postmodernism is not as apparent in the women's writing I explicate. Indeed, *Orlando* is exemplary for its allowance for distinct interpretations through different lenses.

The novella's third-person narrator manipulates readers' expectations; though omniscient, the speaker is an unreliable storyteller, and this innovative approach to narration highlights the characters' human foibles. The biographer tells the titular character's story through varied styles and tones. The short book is a modernist work decades ahead of its time, presaging playful elements of Magical Realism while tackling ideas of gender fluidity and patriarchal oppression. Orlando, a young Elizabethan-era man, inexplicably lives for years without aging and awakens one morning as a female:

> Orlando had become a woman—there is no denying it. However, in every other respect, Orlando's personality remained precisely as it always had been. The change of sex, though it altered their future, did nothing whatever to alter their identity. Their faces remained, as their portraits prove, practically the same. His memory—but in future we must, for convention's sake, say "her" for "his," and "she" for "he"—her memory then, went back through all the events of her past life without encountering any obstacle. (Woolf, 1928, pp. 78–79)

This transformation does not trouble the woman who was once a man; she thrives as a female well into contemporary times. It is fitting that Orlando is an aspiring poet—they have attained aristocratic success as both a male and female, but writing success eludes them. Therefore, *Orlando* straddles omniscient authorship and postmodernist (and modernist) ideas about art, creation, reality, and texts.

2.1.1   "Broken": A Response to Woolf

As an adjunct to *Orlando*, my story "Broken" (collected in *Cherry Bomb*) questions gender roles differently. The dueling third-person narrators and stories lead the two main characters to reconcile after many years; fate brings them back together. Throughout the story, the female character, María-Elena, is a chimpanzee, although this is never explicitly mentioned:

> The train chugged and clattered, and the breeze from the open window fluttered her perfumed hair. She dropped a few grapes into her mouth and burst them one by one, blurring the landscape. She didn't stop eating until she fell asleep.
>   The others in her car didn't have their own bed and pillow. (McGowan, 2024, p. 54)

Readers are not sure why María-Elena is a prisoner. She is in a cage, but at the outset, the reader does not suspect María-Elena is non-human. As the story progresses, the reader recognizes something odd is happening, but cannot locate what makes the story and characters peculiar. María-Elena survives her train crashing, making her way into the woods, her natural forest environment, and discovers her true self.

But is she free? In the end, she seeks and latches onto another keeper. Readers' expectations shift when they discover she is not what they thought she was—the metamorphosis in this piece occurs gradually in the reader's slow realization, unlike Orlando's sudden, unexplainable transition. My story's slow revelation should feel uncomfortable. Hans Shutz is María-Elena's haven, and the two characters attain what they desire most—someone they can love and depend on, which also means they possess no freedom in the confines of their relationship. They are, therefore, *broken*.

2.3   *María Luisa Bombal*

As an exemplar of feminist Magical Realism, María Luisa Bombal's short novel, *The Shrouded Woman*, was first written in Spanish and translated into English by the author. Bombal's work represents an essential step toward creating a feminine literary presence equally critical for Magical Realism, a form dominated by Latino authors. Carlos Fuentes once lauded Bombal, stating, "María Luisa Bombal is the mother of us all" (as cited in Lindstrom, 1995, p. VII). The novella's point-of-view and narration deviate from reality, which relegates the work to Magical Realism. In the novella, Bombal's matriarchal protagonist exists in a state of consciousness between life and death.

With strategically deployed tense and point-of-view shifts coupled with tense imagery, the author depicts the entirety of one woman's life: "She realizes how very often in one's memory only the inflection of a voice or the gesture of a hand remains as a sign of identification of those events which have weighed most heavily on one's destiny" (Bombal, 1995, p. 224). Ana María's inertia as an already-dead protagonist and the various narrators' collective memory (which is inalterable no matter who speaks—all the narrators agree on the same events happening identically) allows for cohesiveness balancing constant shifts of points of view and tenses. Multiple voices anchor the story, allowing the narrative to wash about various consciousnesses in complex interior and exterior lives.

Bombal often employs philosophical commentary: "Men succeed in directing their passion to other things. But the fate of so many women seems to turn over and over in their heart some love sorrow while sitting in a neatly ordered house, facing an unfinished tapestry" (1995, p. 226). The text threads these moments of clarity and retrospect. It does not matter if all the voices in *The Shrouded Woman* are projections of Ana María's consciousness (this would explain how all the events told from disparate perspectives do not include discrepancies). What is essential is that Ana María's life is a web of relationships, and she concludes that she must forgive. As a reader, I grew to admire and forgive Ana María's faults and am inspired to depict my female characters as flawed, human, and boundless.

2.3.1   "Cuts": A Response to Bombal

In my micro-story, "Cuts," which I initially presented as a poem, I try to replicate the sense of regret pervading *The Shrouded Women* (McGowan, 2021a). My tale reimagines the personal stakes of Samson and Delilah's Old Testament story yet within the original tale's bounds/laws (*NJB*, 1985, Judg. 16.4–30). The narrator makes a crucial turn away from the knowns to an immediate moment: the divan, a wine complaint, gossip, the lace curtains, the flitting fingers, spreading hips, and the ornate tunic.

Some details in "Cuts" might underscore Samson's active impotence and effeminacy, but he is only a projection of reality, an eidolon. Delilah explains how Samson's ghost haunts her long after she has seduced and killed him: "My servants held you down. And then I carved out your eyes. Oh, how I've grown to regret my sécateur cuts—you no longer plant seeds inside my kingdom. And fallow fields are useless, aren't they?" (McGowan, 2024, p. 110).

The Philistines betrayed Delilah after she betrayed Samson: They "tricked [her] ... into believing their twined tales" (McGowan, 2024, p. 110). And she is going mad, crippled by the guilt and longing she feels for the man she has killed. When Delilah talks to Samson, she believes he remains in her quarters:

> We lounge in our charnel-like pavilion, and you shift, dry joints creaking on the divan, and you complain about the bitter wine, pinkie hooked as you sip last year's harvest. I comb your ringlets into my loom, gossip about the battles out there, chariot races, army marches you've missed. (McGowan, 2024, p. 110)

In this scene, I attempt to make the phantom of Samson so real that the reader is unsure whether he lives or has already perished. Delilah must face the consequences of her own making until the last sentence, when he lofts off the balcony: "You face the sky, eye sockets escutcheoned, cirrus speeding away, and you fly" (McGowan, 2024, p. 110).

2.4   *Leonora Carrington*

Leonora Carrington's *Complete Stories* (1937–1950s/2017) reveals the themes of her surreal paintings and provides more emotional distance than the emotional rawness of the metaphysically engaged, multivalent narrators in Bombal's *The Shrouded Woman*. Though Carrington is famous as a visual artist, her admirable prose adds another layer to her visual renderings. In her dreamy tales, the outrageous conceits employ dark humor for a complete package. And the imagery is complex—especially Carrington's olfactory descriptions, which are disturbingly redolent.

Outlandishness and grotesqueness proliferate in Carrington's work, yet her detached narrators and characters meet absurd and disturbing events with flippancy or logic. They are so practical—Carrington's people greet supernormal incidents with fortitude. Or indifference. For example, in "Uncle Sam Carrington," a woman witnesses two cabbage heads attack each other, "tearing each other's leaves off with such ferocity" for only the mangled leaves to remain (Carrington, 1937–1938/2017, p. 28). The witness first justifies the violent scene as a terrible dream, but she has not gone to bed yet, so it cannot be a nightmare. Because the story establishes itself as an allegory, revealing the realities of terror and violence indigents experience and endure, especially women, it is also a call to action for change.

2.4.1   "Embrace Light, Admire It, Love It": A Response to Carrington
Though I did not plan to devise a story about a sentient plant, my inspiration
for writing "Embrace light, admire it, love it" (McGowan, 2021b) came from
the time I lived down the street from the George Eastman House in Rochester,
New York. It was a lonely time for me, and I obsessively grew orchids in my
cramped apartment in college. I often heard stories of Eastman's fascination
with plants. But my efforts at cultivation could have been more successful;
usually, an orchid would flower once and never again, so, for years, I walked
around with a question in my head: *What good is a plant that only blooms once?*
A metaphor describing my life. Somehow, I stumbled upon Eastman's struggles
with single-instance-blooming plants in "Embrace light." I made it a love story
and gave the narrator's role to an orchid. But how might a plant speak? How
would it feel to be a plant? I tell the story in one sentence to stress the plant
narrator's eccentric voice.

The breathless narration reveals the freezing orchid's emotional turmoil
as it dies in the greenhouse after an ice storm: "—and you rub my leaves,
half-moaning, *It's no use* ... while I crane to catch your breath's offerings, and
I contemplate the world captured here, the impossible cloched daylight, the
sepia tones give me no hope" (McGowan, 2021b, para. 1). Yes, this is a love story.
The orchid feels special because Eastman has chosen her:

> [—]and you paced, then halted in front of me as you admired my anther
> cap and velvety labellum, your sad eyes gray as an overcast winter morn-
> ing, and you whispered, *Hello, my dear,* and my leaves stiffened at the
> timbre of your voice, and you rubbed a thumb along my spine, your ascot
> wiggling at your throat, blue serge suit lustrous under the chandelier,
> and you proclaimed, *I'll take this Cattleya amethystoglossa,* after which
> you snatched me and departed in haste. (McGowan, 2021b, para. 1)

The story does not end, however.
As the plant dies, the story comes full circle to end with the title's exact
word, rewinding to the first words of the tale:

> [—]and I worry why you won't fire the kerosene heaters or quarter-turn
> our pots or cover us with blankets, why you let this chill steal over our
> rows, why you drag your chair into the dim crevasse between our troughs
> as your lobes and nose turn a new color, your whole face florid from the
> horror as hoarfrost tiptoes inside to nibble on our nodes, and I remember
> your admonition to *embrace light, yes, you must.* (McGowan, 2021b, para. 1)

If the reader circles back to the beginning, they will read the title and the first lines: *"Embrace light, admire it, love it—but above all, know light,* Mr. George Eastman once told me, and so, today, when no warmth remains, I cannot stop thinking of that other February so long ago." Thus, the story is a permanent loop, an infinite life-death cycle.

2.5   *Shirley Jackson*

Shirley Jackson's work lays bare the multiple levels of pressure mid-twentieth century modern women faced as dutiful caretakers and citizens, eschewing the overt surrealism Carrington flaunts or the incipient Magical Realism of Bombal. Indeed, Jackson blends straightforward delivery with surreal or covert horror elements. The allegorical tales collected in her *The Lottery and Other Stories* (1949/1991a) combine domestic settings and surreal elements tinged with the darkness that hangs over proceedings. They are subtle reproaches of society's demands on women. They are also uncanny stories, showing the quotidian to reveal women's inner lives.

Jackson's famous title story, "The Lottery," published in 1948, details a long-established rite culminating in murder, but this story is not wholly indicative of Jackson's oeuvre. The author aims to disquiet rather than shock in her other pieces, underscoring misanthropy and devilish humor, and the threat is often under the surface. Jackson's protagonists are mainly mothers and homemakers. Though her stories frequently combine domestic scenes with understated horror, many are also delicate studies of disillusionment and snobbery—Jackson is a sympathetic, astute observer of domestic life's mundanity: homemaking, feminine disillusionment, and misogyny. References to witchcraft and folklore abound. In "The Witch," an innocuous exchange transpires on a train between a family and a menacing stranger; it becomes a dark conversation, creating layers of ambiguity and confusion for the reader. What is happening? The man admits to the kid a heinous crime that he once chopped up his own sister and ate her. The boy discusses his terror with his mother:

> "Did that man really cut his little sister up in pieces?"
>   "He was just teasing," the mother says and adds urgently, "Just teasing."
>   "Prob'ly," the little boy says. With his lollipop, he went back to his own seat and settled himself to look out the window again. "Prob'ly he was a witch." (Jackson, 1949/1991b, p. 67)

As with many of Jackson's stories, the humdrum reality of daily life metamorphoses into the unfamiliar, never losing sight of black humor and satire.

Ultimately, the reader believes the child's earnest assessment over lending credence to his mother's assurances, which are surprising and disturbing.

Jackson also accomplishes a "haunting" effect in many of her stories by revealing the nastiness and cruelty of ordinary people. The callousness and brutality of "normalcy" in her work allow readers to empathize with Jackson's downtrodden characters; Jackson also forces readers to assess their personal beliefs and conditions. In the title story, "The Lottery," a Vermont hamlet is complicit in a recurring monstrous act; the town holds a drawing to determine who will be stoned to death in the town's ancient ritual, a sacrifice participants believe will ensure a bountiful harvest: "Lottery in June, corn be heavy soon" (Jackson, 1948/1991, p. 297).

At the story's beginning, the omniscient third-person narrator's distance hints at what is building on this "clear and sunny" day in June (Jackson, 1949/1991a, p. 291). The villagers converse about mundanities, "tractors and taxes" in the town square (Jackson, 1948/1991, p. 185), and the children play—a quintessential American scene. Metaphors aside, the story's gory premise ambushes readers drawn into a pastoral All-American setting.

When the town turns on one of its own, it stones her death. Of course, Tessie Hutchinson, the woman stoned by the mob, epitomizes a middle-class American homemaker. Of course, the third-person narrator introduces Tessie into the plot as she washes dishes. And, of course, Tessie is expendable. Indeed, Jackson's lottery does not create lucky winners who squeal, "I'm going to Disneyland!" Instead, it concludes with Tessie frantically protesting, "It isn't fair, it isn't right" (Jackson, 1948/1991, p. 302). But she and the readers are the only people who deem the lottery wrong and evil. Jackson is devastatingly effective in her critiques of American groupthink values and the obliging cruelty undergirding suburban life. Women's roles and lack of agency are emblematic of Jackson's pervasive themes of paternalistic society scapegoating women.

2.5.1   "Four Out of Five Dentists" and "Jump or Dive": Two Responses to
          Jackson

While my story, "Four Out of Five Dentists," is a more overt (and darkly comic) send-up of a serial-killing dentist (Dr. Todd—a tip of my hat to Sweeney Todd), I use similar suspenseful Jacksonian machinations (McGowan, 2018b). I also highlight how evil and cruelty may exist in everyday transactions such as teeth cleaning. The reader feels unsettled throughout the story, but only understands the dentist's evil and callousness at the end after the second-person narrator describes the escape of his patient/victim:

Mrs. Higginbotham's bulging purse sits lonely in the corner, crowding the space. With two pincer fingers, you cram the ugly thing under the sink with all the others.

Then you open the instrument drawer and stow your special scalpel, the serrated one you save for special patients. You intercom the front desk.

"Miss Sadie, can you call the tow company?"

"Yes, Dr. Todd. And your next patient's here."

Fluoride never works. Death may come for our teeth first, but it comes. One out of five dentists agrees. (McGowan, 2018b, p. 47)

Who is scarier than a dentist? Who can be more monstrous? Other narratives in my collection also work to build a feeling of dread and terror; they include "Routine Cleaning" (another evil dentist tale [I dread visits to the dentist]), "The World Will Blow" (a postal employee goes postal), and "Proof Through the Night" (a female officer must lower the Capitol's flag to half-mast after mass shootings).

In "Jump or Dive," another story in *Cherry Bomb*, I tackle themes of family neglect and how children develop self-reliance without supervision. Without supervision, the siblings in the story create their games. Jackson uses ritual in "The Lottery" to reveal her characters' personalities, and I attempt the same in "Jump or Dive" by featuring a ritualistic game the children play each night:

Their favorite game was Cheat the Devil. And though she was younger, Marin was better at it.

"When you Cheat the Devil, you never die, and you don't have to wash the potatoes growing behind your ears," Carter said. The babysitter, Loretta, ignored them and yawned as she sat on the floor, hiking her sweatpants to her knees and swishing the remote in the television's direction, flipping channels between *In Search Of* and *The Cosby Show*.

"When you Cheat the Devil, you live in the dark. You never burp. You walk without legs. It doesn't matter anyway, though, because the Devil can't catch you," Carter continued.

The babysitter stifled another yawn with her elongated splinter of a hand.

"Come now, you two, hit the hay."

Marin walked to the cold fireplace and stood inside it. She clambered higher so Carter and the babysitter could only spy the soles of her shoes dangling from within.

"We see you!" Carter said. ... Loretta made her case.

"When you Cheat the Devil, you have to be good, or the angels won't protect you."

"But this house is already haunted," replied Carter.

"I know. Go to bed." (McGowan, 2024, pp. 124–125)

In this creepy game scene, I attempt to reveal the bond and competition between a brother and sister and how they deal with an outsider, a babysitter. Sure, it is an odd way for kids to play, but I aimed to make it not too spooky, leveraging this scene to build a sense of dread for the reader.

Yes, the house is haunted. But how and why? Ghosts and regret can haunt a person, and this combination is what I attempt with narrative distance created by a third-person point-of-view and the slow revealing of details compounding the growing suspense. Readers sense something is wrong; I fashion emotional space in this scene without exposition. And I only note topical details—the fireplace, the game (how does anyone cheat the Devil, after all?), the young girl and boy tricking their babysitter, and the absence of parental influence. And so, this scene provides a sub-text for the entire story and enriches it with sneaky clues.

2.6   *Lorrie Moore*

Shirley Jackson's stories critique home life and women's societal roles while evoking a subtle sense of horror and unease, while Lorrie Moore's stories indict society's expectations of women. In *Self-Help*, Moore connects the individual tales through their cohesive tone and themes, and her modern, second-person narrators involve the audience in her "how-to" format (1985b). However, the discrete narrators' most salient common trait is their unflinching search for meaning. The imperative voices throughout not only offer instructions to "you" for discovering meaning in the 1980s in middle-class lives, but they also explore and question limited avenues accorded to women for fulfilling lives, including the paths of work, motherhood, daughterhood, sex, intimacy, and language. These females challenge loneliness and isolation by attempting to connect with kith and kin; characters are victims of making bad choices in a seriocomic "how to" fashion.

"How to Become a Writer," the most anthologized story in the collection, advises "you" in an ironic meta-fictional way about the "unfortunate habit" of writing: "Fail miserably. It is best if you fail at an early age—say, fourteen. Early, critical disillusionment is necessary" (Moore, 1985a, p. 119). The narrator, Francie, "you," is engaging because she implicates the reader in the relationship of reader and writer, blurring the line with the reader in which "you" finds "yourself" swept into Francie's life of struggle as an author. Of course, Moore's work drips with satire, the tongue-in-cheek style of a "self-help" book. But there is depth here, too, a looming sense of tragedy in each story—the collection's second-person narrators hector and boss and bluster.

2.6.1   "Cherry Bomb": A Response to Moore

The role of a second-person narrator can be nuanced and intriguing. In "Cherry Bomb" (McGowan, 2019b), the most autobiographical piece in my most recent collection with the same title, Francie is a misfit, eschewing traditional gender roles trapping her:

> Unwilling to pay dues to the Future Homemakers of America, with no interest in pumps or purses, not giving a damn what X stood for, not caring if you could solve for Y, your senior year went south at Zeno High.
>
> You threw out the pasty-pale lipstick your mother gave you while the other girls, those karma chameleons, lounged in their pink bedrooms, Culture Club and Wham! posters plastering their walls. After school, you cherry-bombed your black-lit bedroom, switched on your boom box, and cranked the Dead Kennedys, thrashing to "Holiday in Cambodia," your hairbrush a microphone as you sang and stalked across the imaginary stage like Iggy Pop, the slam-dancing audience chanting your name: *Frankie, Frankie, Frankie.* (McGowan, 2019b, paras. 1–2)

Francie runs away to escape her parents' judgment and society's expectations, only to experience the same problems on the lam. She hitchhikes south:

> But you were careful. You wore a bulky jacket and only thumbed short rides. You didn't tell drivers your age and gripped a steak knife in your pocket just in case.
>
> Borders meant nothing.
>
> Distances measured on maps and dotted boundaries were merely suggestions to you. (McGowan, 2019b, paras. 8–10)

It soon dawns on the second-person narrator how Francie cannot run away from limitations placed on women, on "you."

Her ennui and restlessness are not a reaction to women's appointed roles, but a symptom of life without connections and love:

> In the bright light of day, when you were realistic about it, you knew nobody was looking for you.

> Riding the Greyhound that year, you knew your parents never waited
> by the phone for some trooper to call saying, We found your daughter in
> a ditch. (McGowan, 2019b, paras. 15–16)

The second-person narrator thus inspires an empathetic reaction from
the reader: Francie will never escape what she resents as she searches for
acceptance.

2.7 Angela Carter

Angela Carter's florid and fantastical retelling of fairy tales counters Lorrie
Moore's realist-adjacent characterizations. Carter's characters cannot escape
their human fallibility in the stories collected in *The Bloody Chamber and
Other Stories* (1979b). As feminist retellings of fairy tales, the book's thought-
provoking stories effectively explore gender and power dynamics.

In her interrogations of traditional narratives, Carter blends feminist ideas
of emancipation with supernatural terror. It is haunting. Her exquisite (and
sometimes overwrought) prose truly transports readers to fantastical realms.
However, the juxtaposition of truly human characters trapped in extraordinary
circumstances sheds light on what Carter really wants to convey: Storytelling
has immense transformative power.

Drawing from her perspective as a woman, Carter subverts traditional feminine archetypes and presents protagonists who boldly embrace their desires,
wielding their sexuality as a source of strength. She challenges fairy tales'
societal constructs and moral lessons, urging readers to question norms and
embrace their true selves.

One of the standout stories in this collection is the title piece, "The Bloody
Chamber," a dark and sensual retelling of the Bluebeard tale that delves into
themes of identity and agency as the protagonist navigates her own dark nature;
she is a wife, but not quite, and must confront her primal desire to survive:

> And I began to shudder, like a racehorse before a race, yet also with a
> kind of fear, for I felt both a strange, impersonal arousal at the thought
> of love and at the same time a repugnance I could not stifle for his white,
> heavy flesh that had too much in common with the armfuls of arum lilies
> that filled my bedroom in great glass jars, those undertakers' lilies with
> the heavy pollen that powders your fingers as if you had dipped them in
> turmeric. The lilies I always associate with him; that are white. And stain
> you. (Carter, 1979a, p. 15)

The bride will not submit, and she will prevail.

In Carter's twisted retelling of Little Red Riding Hood, "The Company of Wolves," the female hero defies conventional notions of innocence. She is cunning and self-possessed rather than a victim. As narrated by a third person, the story reveals that the maiden is fully aware of her power and is unafraid to wield it. Like the bride in the story "The Bloody Chamber," the protagonist's knife possession symbolizes her ability to protect herself. As Carter writes, "She has her knife and she is afraid of nothing" (Carter, 1979c, p. 114). The phallic nature of the knife also reverses roles.

And finally, in "The Tiger's Bride," readers encounter a variation of the story of Beauty and the Beast with its theme of self-discovery. At the end of the tale, the Beast seduces the female first-person narrator, and through her surrender, she undergoes a radical transformation:

> He dragged himself closer and closer to me, until I felt the harsh velvet of his head against my hand, then a tongue, abrasive as sandpaper. 'He will lick the skin off me!'
> And each stroke of his tongue ripped off skin after successive skin, all the skins of a life in the world, and left behind a nascent patina of shining hairs. My earrings turned back to water and trickled down my shoulders; I shrugged the drops off my beautiful fur. (Carter, 1979d, p. 67)

After her alteration into a beast, the protagonist transforms into an unfamiliar creature altogether and experiences freedom and confidence. True love is not the goal, a thematic reversal of the classic tale. What I enjoy about Carter's work is that it invites us to look beyond the surface of the familiar to question and dream, to find truth in the fantastic.

2.7.1   "The World's Full of Murderers": Response to Carter

As I explore the possibilities of storytelling, I often use fairy tale conventions to highlight social conditions, echoing Carter's ruminations and thematic obsessions with classic tropes. However, when my tales depart from reality, I do not depend on more obvious notions of fabulism. As an illustration, in my tale, "The World's Full of Murderers" (collected in *Cherry Bomb*), I allegorize human callousness after a disaster, pitting a maiden against a hag.

Ava senses growing danger as she realizes that the unnamed older woman did not rescue her when she was scooped into a life raft. The older woman sits inside a tented tarp on the post-stamp-sized vessel and is never completely visible. The lack of visual clarity for Ava adds to the story's progressing menace, mainly because only parts of her body are visible: "The woman held both hands outside her tent, her left hand gesticulating wildly at the sky while the

right hand gripped the knife tight and aimed it toward Ava, the blade glinting"
(McGowan, 2024, p. 107).

This story is an opportunity to explore social contract notions and study
how humans care for one another. The narrativization explicates lifeboat ethics at its most extreme with the story's implicit question: Should a person save
others if it might jeopardize their well-being?

The story opens with Ava on a yacht, her passage paid for by her uncle; she
is concerned about not identifying a suitable subject for her unwritten novel.
In her quest for an engaging topic for the non-existent book she has not even
begun writing, she pauses ridiculously to reflect on a striking line as her ship
sinks: "And besides, *in sleep, people are blind*." She would have to remember the
line for her book—in sleep, people are blind. What an *à propos* chapter title
(McGowan, 2024, p. 97). The boat goes down, but Ava survives and awakens on
an inflatable raft. She knows nothing about sailing, fishing, or the ocean. Her
willing ignorance about survival skills and her lack of writing abilities echo
many aspects of Dr. Brannigan's hubris in "Two Trees" (also collected in *Cherry
Bomb*); sanctimonious white feminists get taken down a few notches in my
work.

Ava is shipwrecked and knows she is going to die if the woman in the life raft
will not help her: "Ava thought about what the woman was to her. She'd pulled
her from the water like a fish. And she'd let her die of thirst. The woman had
saved her once and could save her again if she chose. She was at once a rescuer
and a judge" (McGowan, 2024, p. 107). However, as they continue to languish
on the raft, Ava knows there is no opportunity to escape:

> "So, you're going to let me die?" Ava asked incredulously.
>
> "I'm not letting you die," the woman responded coolly. "You will die as
> you die. As a body will."
>
> "Why save me then? Why'd you pull me into this raft?"
>
> "I didn't mean to save you," said the woman. "I didn't think you'd live,
> so I didn't truly save you."
>
> She cleared her throat and drummed her fingernails on the raft, keep-
> ing time. "It's more like ... I caught you. And you're the first thing I've
> caught in weeks."
>
> Now, the woman's intentions were obvious to Ava. (McGowan, 2024,
> p. 105)

Indeed, Ava is no more to the woman than a fish reeled onto the raft.

As the story shifts in the middle to highlight a debate between Ava and the
unnamed woman, the dialogue pits deontology against utilitarianism. Ava
continues to explain how she is a writer, which the woman meets with disdain.

However, Ava persists, reminiscing about a recent romantic encounter on her ship before it sank, and the menacing woman interrupts:

> "Hush," she said harshly. "I don't want to hear this story. I know this story and don't want to hear it anymore."
> "How do you know this story?"
> "It's anybody's story. You think you're the only one to fuck? It's as familiar as the shape of this raft, and it's making me bored and hungry."
> But Ava kept talking, not caring what the woman wanted. The tale wasn't original but hers, and she'd tell it come Hell or high water. (McGowan, 2024, p. 108)

Utilitarianism, blind brutality, and the Devil in the guise of an older woman win out, dashing storytelling's possibilities for healing and emancipation. "The World Is Full of Murderers" is a fairy tale with no happy conclusion; it is a morality tale, a fable, the anti-*One Thousand and One Arabian Nights*.

2.8   *Kelly Link*

If Angela Carter uses Fabula to question feminine roles in our existence and reality-adjacent places, Kelly Link's grotesqueries and fantastical worlds in *Stranger Things Happen* (2001a) are a soupçon of contemporary authenticity. Link prefers an impersonal tone with nonlinear storytelling techniques, but she compels readers to the emotional experiences. The dynamic content of her stories derives from a sense of identification readers experience when reading her damaged characters. These people (especially children) attempt to put on brave faces amid chaotic and terrifying alternative worlds.

Echoing Carter's style, Link's "Travels with the Snow Queen" explores themes of love, betrayal, and self-discovery through a complex narrative structure and dreamlike imagery. The second-person narration centers on Gerda, a young woman whose partner is taken by the infamous Snow Queen. Her journey is less about rescuing him than regaining her sense of self.

The narrative is a hilarious send-up peppered with witty remarks, insightful critiques about how traditional fairy tales portray women merely as rewards for male protagonists despite their ordeals, and sharp, humorous comments, such as a fanciful idea about starting a travel service for these fairy-tale women. Gerda grapples with her desires and autonomy: "Part of you is always traveling faster, always traveling ahead. Even when you are moving, it is never fast enough to satisfy that part of you" (Link, 2001b, p. 99). Such a postmodernist story reimagines a classic fairy tale and serves as a profound commentary on the quest for identity and empowerment in a fractured world that often sees women through a reductive lens.

However, "Vanishing Act" is perhaps the most haunting tale in the collection. Through the perspective of a young girl trying to feel connected to her apathetic family, Link employs striking imagery to reveal deeply rooted issues: "The chair where she sits at the dinner table is like the space at the back of the mouth ... where the feeling of possessing a tooth still lingers" (Link, 2001c, p. 132). Gritty truths belie Link's lyrical prose, inviting readers to contemplate the themes of familial detachment with the girl's body parts gradually detaching, a literal detachment in a family with no grounding.

Stranger Things Happen's stories show how the fantastic can illustrate human complexities. Through their unconventional structures and profound emotional landscapes, the narratives in Stranger Things challenge readers to reconsider and perhaps even redraw the boundaries between reality and imagination, ordinary and extraordinary.

2.8.1 "Reservoir": A Response to Link

Kelly Link is at her strongest when exposing her characters' interior lives and coping mechanisms as they confront absurdities and endure surreal, impossible circumstances they attempt to normalize. In my story, "Reservoir" (McGowan, 2019e), a plural first-person narrator speaks for two young brothers dealing with loss; they seem more like a singular entity: "We don't talk; we aim at corners and fight beasts. All our sounds vanish into slammed closets. The quiet drifts through our house graceful as a canoe, seaworthy, rotatable. Overturned. Possibilities haunt the stairs, descending" (McGowan, 2019e, para. 12). With such a unique point-of-view, I attempt to interpret what happens when sadness is so overwhelming that the self fractures, losing its individuality. What can the boys do but try to lean on each other and pool their consciousnesses?

From the outset, the reader comprehends how the boys have lost their grip on reality or how something more miraculous is happening:

> Sometimes, we climb into the cracked shell of our drained swimming pool. Inside its leaf-filled cavity with its waterlogged piles, half-slimy, half-frozen, we pretend we're ocean superheroes and battle a make-believe shark as it circles the concrete cavern. (McGowan, 2019e, para. 2)

Childhood is a time of magical moments full of play and made-up games. But there is more meaning to these characters' flights of fancy: their sister died in the same pool.

"Reservoir" is the only story in my collection where the females at the narrative's heart exist off-stage, influencing others' actions passively. Yes, feminine specters loom over the protagonists and their father—an absent mother who has run off and a tragically killed sister: "After the funeral, Mom drove away in the old station wagon, and we haven't seen her since. … Dad has quick-sanded into himself. He wears soft shoes and shuffles across the hard floors upstairs" (McGowan, 2019e, paras. 11, 13). By examining the concept of grief as an actual haunting, I attempt to explain how a child experiences the death of an immediate family member. Authoring this story was a way to come to terms with my father's death—he passed when I was nine, my life riven in two at the news of his accident, a real-life before and after.

The story ends as the boys, who have developed into wildlings with no adult supervision, listen to their father mourning:

> We worry Dad doesn't know we're here. Every night, after I tell Jon to pray, we tuck in, and after I pull my greasy sheets to my chin, we hear Dad scuffle across the floorboards in the hallway. And there are thudding sounds as if somebody's trapped in the belly of a whale drifting far away, deep under the sea. Dad's skeleton keys rattle on a ring, and he jiggles the locked doors' handles, swings them open one by one, and whispers *goodnight* to somebody we can't see. (McGowan, 2019e, para. 23)

Each person handles grief and sadness differently, but imagination is a comfort, especially for the children in "Reservoir."

2.9   *"Women on Top": My Other Stories*

The *Weibermacht*, translated as "the power of women" in German, is an artistic trope common in Western civilization's creative works, mainly Northern European Renaissance paintings. The art historian Susan L. Smith originally coined the term in *The Power of Women: A "Topos" in Medieval Art and Literature* (1995); she posits *Weibermachtian* concepts might reveal a more nuanced understanding of representations of women in art:

> In appealing to examples of famous women who caused the suffering of the men who loved them too well, … [*the Weibermacht*] *topos* is just one of many manifestations of the medieval preoccupation with women who seize the upper hand in their relations with men. … What distinguishes the Power of Women *topos* and gives it its particular impact is that it singles out the most celebrated men of the past to prove the power of women. … [I]n every instance, the *topos*'s purpose is the same: to bring to bear the authority of history on the issue of women and power. (p. 2)

While the *Weibermacht topos* initially warned viewers about giving women too much control, the form's unintended meaning now allows feminists to even the score. I, too, intend this.

Smith explores the topic a couple of decades later in her 2015 essay "Woman on Top," in which the *Weibermacht* "brings together two or more famous examples from the Bible, ancient history, and romance to prove that women can master even the worthiest of men" (Smith, 2015, p. 845). Of course, the double entendre is intriguing because the term's common parlance refers to sexual intercourse. Smith also entertains the idea's emancipatory possibilities of a "Woman on Top" in her short essay, explaining she adapted her title from Nancy Z. Davis's essay "Women on Top" (1975), which examines women who "dress as men and play male roles" (Smith, 2015, p. 844). The Power of Women tropes depict women gaining the upper hand over men, drawing on artistic representations of women straddling men so she can expand the *Weibermacht*'s meaning. This trope, however, is only enacted through violence or physical prowess. However, there is more going on than male-female role reversals. The traditional works of art warn viewers of how uncontrollable women pose a mortal danger to societal norms; this countering of traditional gender dynamics creates jarring and fascinating imagery, with the surprise shift in power relations a novel concept for such early works.

While I may not write scenes of violence or advocate for physical domination, most of my story depictions include women's psychological struggles to come out "on top." My female characters might wish they were subjects of *Weibermacht* paintings (if they knew what they were). Contemporary portrayals of gender often imply how male power is indestructible and permanent, how women cannot be heroic and are ornaments or derive their power from men. In predominantly male-leaning media, one must act more like a man to perform better than a man. Or become one. In my fiction, I subvert this certainty and lean toward a *Weibermachtian* feeling, celebrating femininity apart from masculinity.

My female heroes and anti-heroes yearn to be as powerful, if not more so, than their male counterparts, aiming to overcome their relegation to the sidelines. By retelling the Samson and Delilah Bible tale from Delilah's perspective, my most *Weibermachtian* story, "Cuts" (McGowan, 2021a), makes us comprehend (almost) a monstrous act committed by a misguided person. And though readers may not endorse emasculating and blinding someone, they know why Delilah acted. Her violence feels inevitable, though we have entered her story *in medias res*—the haircutting and eye gouging happened years before.

In another take on a Bible tale, "Manger," I am more subtle, imbuing a modern-day Virgin Mary with a different, less decisive lack of autonomy. Though

Christian and Islamic doctrine claim God asexually impregnated Mary to conceive Jesus and Mary's impregnation was consensual, I am not confident she was completely willing. Who says no to God? Thus, if Mary had no control over becoming the mother of Jesus or could have avoided the pain of giving birth to someone claiming to be the Messiah, in my version, she might have escaped the demons chasing her.

Several of my characters figuratively decapitate their oppressors. If only it were as simple in our daily lives, where hegemonic structures continue to limit women's possibilities. In "The World Will Blow" (McGowan, 2020e), a postal clerk turns to violence, but instead of taking out her local mail branch, she bombs a bank. I originally made this antagonist a male, but after publication, I could not resist changing "him" to "her." But what drives anyone to such murderous extremes? This postal worker explodes the bank vault after electrical currents possess her, and she kills her girlfriend: "The cricket hum's silent where the body's disappeared" (McGowan, 2020e, para. 1). And the clerk feels no remorse or hesitation.

Because my anti-heroes obviate or obliterate the prevailing conditions of society, they are less sympathetic to the reader. My goal is to challenge perceptions of what is possible for females. If readers only focus on my female characters' external circumstances, perceiving them as slightly whacky, solidly angry, or outright evil, labeling them monstrous. However, these characters do the best they can.

In "A Sword Is a Question," I create a mythic world in which the main character, Brynhild, kills her rapist and becomes a Valkyrie: "Brynhild … faces the dawn's red riot and waits for her sisters to carry her far away from these people and their angry mountain, their falling men" (McGowan, 2018c, para. 37). A newer story, in the early draft stage and tentatively titled "Bandit, Bank Robber, Thief," explores petty crimes and major illegal acts and how lawbreakers may have reasons for their actions: "This is crazy—someone must go out for cheese or toothpaste or whatnot. The rent's overdue. Our path to ruination is mutually assured. So inevitable and clichéd. Mundane. And any life can surge south." Perhaps my criminals are trying to survive as best they can in a cruel world. Regardless of any offenders' intentions, we should treat them respectfully.

• • •

While I am not dismissive of my other stories (I have only mentioned half the pieces in *Cherry Bomb*), many of my works remain unexamined in this book's contextualization. However, they are my most essential or engaging pieces. They are also more challenging for me to write about or describe. Am I too

close to my characters? Yes, but I put them through the wringer. My protagonists suffer and are self-destructive or lack self-awareness, the closest psychi-
cally to who I am.

Nonetheless, I show that women are as capable of monstrous acts as men.
However, someone acting evil does not make them evil, and I try to reveal the
catalysts forcing my characters to act out and impart harm. "Heretic" presents
Connie, an active narcotics user who has spiraled into a dark place (McGowan,
2019c). She is pregnant with no options. On a walk one afternoon, as she
waits for her connection, she encounters a tree, the site of a nasty breakup.
She torches the oak, which is unforgivable, but what redeems her is how she
remains tender toward her beloved cat: "In the tree, crackles give way to roars.
She pats Elbert, who is shifting and whining, backs away from the pyrotech-
nics, turns, strides home. The rhythm of her pace calms him, and he slackens"
(McGowan, 2019c, p. 112). Indeed, one cannot define Connie as monstrous or
loving because she is such a complex character.

My story, "The Sheriff's Deputy Who Transported Me," is the most painful
story I have ever written—it depicts a first-person narrator who has attempted
suicide and is being moved to a long-term mental facility. Then there are my
stories that tackle complex romantic problems, including "Never Salute a
Bare Head," "Any Other Thursday," "The Sympathy of Clocks," and "Love Is a
Graveyard for the Lonely" (McGowan, 2024). The human need for connection
is a theme in my work. In "Lookers," I riff on *Thelma and Louise* (McGowan,
2021c). If anyone has watched the movie, they know the titular characters cast
off the constraints of society's expectations—they are feminist ideals. The
women shift from "good little housewives" to outlaws and drive over a cliff's
edge to escape capture.

However, in my story, unlike the movie, the women do not need a suicide
pact; instead, the two outlaw women travel through the desert with no active
law enforcement presence chasing them. Thelma, the narrator, describes their
modus operandi: "Louise and I prefer a night-time ramble to the straight shot
of freeways or the whiz-by of eighteen-wheelers. Or the possibility of a trooper
on the median. She reminds me that Texas is always off-limits. I admire these
lonely places as we lattice routes through one-horse podunks, the vacancy
signs spilling neon shadows across two-laners" (McGowan, 2021c, p. 1). Thelma
and Louise try to get by as lovers and embrace the freedom of no more ties to a
suburban existence; they reject a male-dominated society. The women are not
monsters; they are misunderstood.

The qualities we praise as heroic in Western culture—courage and fortitude, selflessness and nobility, steadfastness and will—are not unique to men.
They are not necessarily characteristic of men, yet society labels these qualities

as masculine. Media promoting misogyny has defined our culture and controlled the grand narrative for centuries. Those interested in change struggle to create or consume stories about valorous women because most of these tales also depict "feminine" virtues: passivity and fragility requiring rescue. Any hero embodying a role outside accepted norms also plants the seeds of her undoing. I intend to change this. I plan to devise imperfect and heroic female characters as I endeavor forward—more imperfect and courageous than my current women. My female heroes are often incapable of shirking the shackles of femininity, unable to break free from society's limitations, but they still go places. I long to liberate my female characters.

Women do not have it easy, whether we are going about our everyday lives. Society considers us as equals only when it is convenient or expedient; when we try to exert control or power over our destinies, it brands us as malcontents or monsters. If life appears normal on the surface, or if a female is boring or too staid, can she break free and transcend society's limitations? And if she can break free, will there be consequences for her? If a woman gains agency, there is no guarantee that she will not face mockery, infantilization, or demonization for her attempts.

True transcendence is a fantasy; perfect outcomes seldom occur in real life and, more rarely, in my fiction. The best way forward with my future writing enterprises is to go all in and tap into women's unique roles in contemporary society, embracing the monstrous. Misogynistic norms often relegate independent or powerful women to monster roles, so why not manipulate misguided opinions warning against ambition, ugliness, voracious appetites, and vicious wrath? My work resists resolutions and embraces messy outcomes and monsters.

Ancient Greek artists often depicted Medusa as non-threatening, fashioning statues of her with a shapely body. Yet folks knew it was inadvisable to brush her hair. I aim to embrace monsters' roles and turn them upside down by writing Weibermachts. I want to brush Medusa's hair and not suffer the consequences men do. We need more female heroes in fiction who are monstrosities, women who break through gendered notions of who may embody courage and strength. Female demons and grossly exaggerated personas might provide an innovative approach to heroism for a society obsessed with feminine ideals.

2.9.1   "Certain Smile": A Magical Realist Response

Arguably, the most iconic story in Western culture is the Bible's New Testament, an epic tracing the birth, life, death, and resurrection of Jesus Christ—Christianity's core tenets are based on the notion that God the Father sent His Son to Earth to take corporeal form, to live as a human, die as a human, and return from the dead so He might open a pathway to Heaven for human souls. For believers, Jesus's Resurrection proved He is the Messiah and Son of God. His rising from the dead can also be interpreted as the most influential magical realist piece ever.

Of course, I cannot compete with divine magic, but I can examine the ideas of resurrection and transmogrification. I prefer referencing a less consequential resurrection: the Lazarus story (*New Jerusalem Bible* [*NJB*], 1985, John 11:1–44). In my story, "Certain Smile" (McGowan, 2019a), an innocent and neglected girl discovers she can bring back to life the dead and transform a perished boy into a bird merely after touching his corpse:

The boy disappears. He transmogrifies into another thing altogether. His true self.

> Now, you cup a cardinal in your palm, though his neck lolls to the side like a wilted flower stem; his mouth's a beak splintered in two places. Then, the creature's muscles soften as his head rights itself, the beak cracks disappear, and your trance ends with the movement. The now-warm feathered thing trembles, opens his dusky eyes, shudders, perches his wiry feet on your finger, and shakes his revivified wings. (McGowan, 2019a, paras. 27–28)

Although the main action and scene in this story is the restoration of a child's life, it is not the tale's centerpiece, but a side-effect of how the girl suffers from parental neglect.

The second-person narrator also directly engages the reader, asking them to internalize what it is to possess the supernatural gift of resurrecting the dead. It may sound blasphemous, but I want readers to consider how they might positively influence and change others' destinies, an essential theme in many of my stories. My Magical Realism allows for the possibility of defeating inevitable death with a miracle: "Off he flies, and as the red blur lofts skyward over the leaf-strewn roadway, he shits on your parents' arriving limousine circling the building's drive" (McGowan, 2019a, para. 33).

2.9.2   "Manger": Another Magical Realist Response
A framing technique of tongue-in-cheek meta-construction, my story "Manger" calls into question the origin story of Christianity with its contemporary mash-up of zombie and nativity stories (*NJB*, 1985, Luke 1–2). It is also a spin on how fairy tales and stories are told and passed down to future listeners and readers—the narrator controls the drama. The story begins:

People die, but why start any story with an ending? Grief's a better plot point—grief is as painful ten or twenty years after a death, perhaps more so, as it was in the first moment of loss. But stories must end. Right?

This story isn't explicable yet, or at least not before a miracle saves a narrator from killing the characters or breaking their hearts. Or yours.

Somebody must tell the story.

It's about a woman, man, and newborn under an unfriendly sun inside a desert near a dried-up river in a sheltered clearing. They're fugitives. They're figures of devotion. They're fictions of characterization, of purpose, of loss in the days before cell phone towers, before television screens flickered in each home, before computers spat out information no one needs.

Of course, starting a story with any dread or death creates other problems; there's no good place to begin, but someone must tell this tale. (McGowan, 2024, p. 77)

And so pregnant Mary gives birth in a broken-down Caprice, a horde of demons descends upon the family:

Mary's head shone, and the pivoting planets above in a brightening sky orbited that harsh nativity. And Mary and Joseph waited for their baby's arrival as she pushed through her pain. He held her hand.

Then, the two first spied wraiths, diminutive demons, mere specters drifting from behind a rise on the highway's other side. The see-through forms advanced and grew enormous. (McGowan, 2024, p. 80)

Thus, my fusion of reality and cynical narration reveals my postmodernist leanings. The uncanny elements present difference and oddness—magical stories question the nature of reality.

2.9.3   "Poppies": A Fabulist Response

I filter fantastic theoretical ideas through my feminine lens in my current writing practice. Though I never sit down to pen a story with specific approaches in mind, I can detect the concepts from my reading seep into my narratives. I internalize resonant ideas. My story "Poppies" (McGowan, 2020b) presents a collage of these influences. Initially, I found inspiration in a newspaper human interest piece about a bear who broke into a house, a caper captured on security cameras as the bear sat at the homeowner's piano and plunked on the keys as if it knew how to make music. The incident haunted me for a few years; The first sentence of "Poppies" relays how much real estate the bear occupied in my consciousness: "I couldn't shake the bear" (McGowan, 2020b, para. 1).

As I fleshed out the story over months, my first-person narrator, an unfulfilled woman coping with an abusive relationship, becomes fixated on the bear who appears to her only in dreams. I draw on my life experiences. The tension builds as uncertainty increases, and the reader is unsure about what is real and what is not. The narrator's reliability is also questionable, and the fantastical elements woven throughout the story emphasize a tenuous separation between memory, reality, and imagination. "Poppies" does the work of both feminist and fantastic theories because it departs from verisimilitude to stress the female narrator's tenuous position.

The narrator's dreams of her bear doppelgänger work to heal her, help her overcome her stark reality, and accept what the reader suspects—she is pregnant. The story ends with a fantastical conclusion, a meta-statement about how the story is not over, similar to how my stories "Manger" and "The Odds" (both collected in *Cherry Bomb*) address the nature of plotlines adhering to Freytag's Pyramid (a plot with rising action, a climax, and a resolution): "I know it's a cliché to end a story with, *and then I woke up*, but I did, and this is not an ending, anyway" (McGowan, 2020b, para. 26). By ending my story by employing and acknowledging a tired writing ploy and trying to revivify it, I take the rules to task, as the events in the story blur the lines between reality and dreams.

2.9.4   "Last Days of Men": A Feminist Response

Another of my stories, a culmination of feminist theories and fantastical elements of my other stories, "Last Days of Men," uses modernist collage effects, the disconnected voices adding to a cohesive plot (McGowan, 2020a). In this way, the story mimics or echoes Woolf's nonlinear foci. The different voices, including a first-person plural section, are not necessarily those of a protagonist: "During those sweltering days and the uncomfortable, sticky evenings, we stepped outside to view the phenomenon, to marvel at the flying men as if their antics were an airshow. We sure enjoyed the spectacle—the airborne aces were hams, cheerfully waving when they zoomed past" (McGowan, 2020a, para. 21).

The protagonist witnesses the world's changes with a mixture of bemusement and horror. She, a woman going through a divorce, is traumatized by losing her life with a man and witnessing a changing world where men inexplicably float into the atmosphere to fly around and never return. The metaphorical implications are obvious, but readers are unsure whether this is all in the protagonist's head or if it is accurate. She must accept a now half-empty planet:

> One lady wistfully told her friend, "I'm so *glad* we're not up there."
> We women ambled along the sidewalks. With each step, more females joined us—we vacated apartment buildings and grocery stores; some even abandoned their cars along the road, motors still running, doors open, swinging in the breeze. Our numbers swelled as we spilled onto the streets and paraded away. We were a deliberate herd with no true end-destination, elbowing or pushing, no one striving or jostling or angling for perfection or attention. (McGowan, 2020a, paras. 52–53)

In the end, the protagonist, the last section's first-person narrator, welcomes the drastic absence of men. The story ends on a triumphant feminist note tempered by the devastating, total loss of men.

References

Bal, M. (2009). *Narratology: Introduction to the theory of narrative* (3rd ed.). University of Toronto Press. (Original work published 1985)

Bochner, A. P. (2012, December 31). On first-person narrative scholarship: Autoethnography as acts of meaning. *Narrative Inquiry*, 22(1), 155–164. https://doi.org/10.1075/ni.22.1.10boc

Bombal, M. L. (1995). *House of mist and the shrouded woman: Two novels*. University of Texas Press.

Burke, E. (1958). *A philosophical enquiry into the origin of our ideas of the sublime and beautiful* (J. T. Boulton, Ed.). Columbia University Press. (Original work published 1759)

Carrington, L. (2017). *The complete stories of Leonora Carrington*. Dorothy. (Original work published 1937–1950)

Carrington, L. (2017). Uncle Sam Carrington. In *The complete stories of Leonora Carrington*. Dorothy. (Original work published 1937–1938)

Carter, A. (1979a). The bloody chamber. In *The bloody chamber and other stories* (pp. 7–41). Penguin Books.

Carter, A. (1979b). *The bloody chamber and other stories*. Penguin Books.

Carter, A. (1979c). The company of wolves. In *The bloody chamber and other stories* (pp. 110–118).

Carter, A. (1979d). The tiger bride. In *The bloody chamber and other stories* (pp. 51–67).

Cixous, H. (1976, July). Le rire de la Méduse [The Laugh of the Medusa]. *Signs: Journal of Women in Culture and Society, 1*(4), 875–893. https://doi.org/10.1086/493306

Coleridge, S. T. (2021). Biographia literaria; or biographical sketches of my literary life and opinions. In P. Swaab (Ed.), *Wordsworth* (1st ed., pp. 2–5). Routledge. (Original work published 1834)

Coward, R. (1980, July). "This novel changes lives": Are women's novels feminist novels? A response to Rebecca O'Rourke's article "summer readings." *Feminist Review, 5*(1), 53–64. https://doi.org/10.1057/fr.1980.12

Czerwiec, H. (2018). Using poetic forms in nonfiction. *Assay Journal.* Retrieved March 29, 2024, from https://assayjournal.wordpress.com/2018/11/12/__trashed-2/

Derrida, J. (1981). *Positions* (A. Bass, Trans.). University of Chicago Press.

Doubrovsky, S. (1977). *Fils.* Galilée.

Eagleton, M. (1996). *Working with feminist criticism.* Blackwell Publishers.

Eagleton, T. (2004). *After theory.* Basic Books.

Ettorre, E. (2017). *Autoethnography as feminist method: Sensitising the feminist "I."* Routledge.

Felski, R. (2008). *Uses of literature* (1st ed.). Wiley.

Felski, R. (2015). *The limits of critique.* University of Chicago Press.

Freud, S. (2003). The uncanny (D. McLintock, Trans.). In *The uncanny.* Penguin Books. (Original work published 1919)

Gadamer, H.-G. (1984). The hermeneutics of suspicion. *Man and World, 17*(3-4), 313–323. https://doi.org/10.1007/BF01250456

Gilbert, S. M., & Gubar, S. (1979). *The madwoman in the attic: The woman writer and the nineteenth-century literary imagination.* Yale University Press.

Ginsberg, A. (1999). American sentences 1995–1997. In B. Rosenthal, P. Carroll, & M. Schumacher (Eds.), *Death & fame: Poems 1993–1997* (pp. 79–80). HarperCollins.

Hirsch, E. D., Jr. (2006). Building knowledge. *American Educator, 30*(1), 8–50.

Huehls, M. (2016). *After critique: Twenty-first-century fiction in a Neoliberal age.* Oxford University Press.

Jackson, S. (1991). The lottery. In *The lottery and other stories.* Noonday Press. (Original work published 1948)

Jackson, S. (1991a). *The lottery and other stories.* Noonday Press. (Original work published 1949)

Jackson, S. (1991b). The witch. In *The lottery and other stories.* Noonday Press. (Original work published 1949)

Kant, I. (1951). *Critique of judgement* (J. H. Bernard, Trans.). Hafner. (Original work published 1790)

Leavy, P. (2019, November 22). Fiction, feminism, and qualitative research: An interview with Dr. Patricia Leavy. *The Qualitative Report, 24*(11), 2929–2933. https://doi.org/10.46743/2160-3715/2019.4493

Lindstrom, N. (1995). *Foreword* (M. Bombal, Ed.). University of Texas Press.

Link, K. (2001a). *Stranger things happen*. Small Beer Press.

Link, K. (2001b). Travels with the snow queen. In *Stranger things happen* (pp. 99–120). Small Beer Press.

Link, K. (2001c). Vanishing act. In *Stranger things happen* (pp. 121–143). Small Beer Press.

McGowan, C. (2018a). Depending on the horizon. *Unbroken Journal*(16). Retrieved March 23, 2024, from https://unbrokenjournal.com/2018/01/depending-on-the-horizon-by-cate-mcgowan/

McGowan, C. (2018b). Four out of five dentists agree. *Ellipsis Zine: The Whisper Place*(4), 45–47.

McGowan, C. (2018c). A sword is a question. *Barrelhouse, Fall of Men*. Retrieved March 23, 2024, from https://web.archive.org/web/20190428195334/https://www.barrelhousemag.com/onlinelit/2018/9/24/a-sword-is-a-question

McGowan, C. (2019a). Certain smile. *Barren Magazine*(6). Retrieved March 23, 2024, from https://barrenmagazine.com/certain-smile/

McGowan, C. (2019b). Cherry bomb. *TSS Publishing*. Retrieved March 23, 2024, from https://theshortstory.co.uk/cherry-bomb-by-cate-mcgowan/

McGowan, C. (2019c). Heretic. *Tahoma Literary Review*(15), 109–112. Retrieved March 23, 2024, from https://tahomaliteraryreview.com/issues/issue-15/

McGowan, C. (2019d). Reservoir. *Atticus review*. Retrieved March 23, 2024, from https://atticusreview.org/reservoir-2/

McGowan, C. (2020a). Last days of men. *Phoebe Journal*, *49*(1), 5–11.

McGowan, C. (2020b). Poppies. *Riggwelter*(28). Retrieved March 23, 2024, from https://issuu.com/riggwelter/docs/issue_28

McGowan, C. (2020c). Unrhymed sonnet constructed with American sentences. *Crack the Spine*(266), 4. Retrieved March 23, 2024, from https://pub.lucidpress.com/crackthespine266/#YJUYqZUusL1G

McGowan, C. (2020d). The world will blow. *Unbroken Journal*, *24*. Retrieved March 23, 2024, from https://unbrokenjournal.com/2020/01/catemcgowan/

McGowan, C. (2021a, Fall). Cuts. *The Citron Review*. Retrieved March 23, 2024, from https://citronreview.com/2021/09/23/falling-is-the-deadest-thing-a-cento/

McGowan, C. (2021b). Embrace light, admire it, love it. *Hypertext magazine*(Spring/Summer). Retrieved March 23, 2024, from https://www.hypertextmag.com/and-mister-george-eastman-once-told-me-to-embrace-light-admire-it-love-it-lookers/

McGowan, C. (2021c, Spring/Summer). Lookers. *Hypertext magazine*. Retrieved March 23, 2024, from https://www.hypertextmag.com/and-mister-george-eastman-once-told-me-to-embrace-light-admire-it-love-it-lookers/

McGowan, C. (2024). *Cherry bomb* [Unpublished manuscript].

Miller, B. (2015). The shared space between reader and writer: A case study. *Brevity: A Journal of Concise Literary Nonfiction*. Retrieved March 23, 2024, from https://brevitymag.com/craft-essays/the-shared-space/

Moore, L. (1985a). How to become a writer. In *Self-help: Stories* (pp. 117–126). Warner Books.

Moore, L. (1985b). *Self-help: Stories.* Warner Books.

Mulvey, L. (1975, 1975-09-01). Visual pleasure and narrative cinema. *Screen, 16*(3), 6–18. https://doi.org/10.1093/screen/16.3.6

The new Jerusalem Bible (H. Wansbrough, Trans.). (1985). Doubleday.

Ricœur, P. (2008). *Freud and philosophy: An essay on interpretation* (D. Savage, Trans.). Yale University Press.

Rosenblatt, L. (1985, 1985). Transaction versus interaction: A terminology rescue operation. *Research in the Teaching of English, 19*, 96–107.

Showalter, E. (2011). *Gilbert and Gubar's The madwoman in the attic after thirty years.* University of Missouri Press.

Smith, S. L. (1995). *The power of women: A topos in medieval art and literature.* University of Pennsylvania Press.

Smith, S. L. (2015). Woman on top. In M. Schaus (Ed.), *Women and gender in medieval Europe: An encyclopedia* (pp. 844–845). Taylor & Francis.

Stein, G. (2012). *Tender buttons: Objects, food, rooms.* Dover Publications. (Original work published 1914)

Todorov, T. (1975). *The fantastic: A structural approach to a literary genre.* Cornell University Press.

Woolf, V. (1928). *Orlando: A biography.* Hogarth Press.

Worthington, M. (2018). *The story of "me": Contemporary American autofiction.* University of Nebraska Press.

CHAPTER 11

Coda

In this collection of disparate essays, I have tried to answer the questions beginning this work: How might my composition of short fiction facilitate my ability to write "truthful stories"? And how does my work express my innermost truths as it reveals circumstances limiting women's autonomy? My writing reflects the impact of my journey as a female and my efforts to make a difference as I examine the truths of my life.

I am attempting to fuse many disparate elements (my own Frankenstein's monster) in my criticism, contextualization, and creative endeavors, but my fusion attempts to realize cohesion. However, my characters are not chess pieces; they are wind-up dolls acting unexpectedly. My fictional expressions and implementations of feminist protest attempt to tap effectively into the various theories influencing me as I reveal the humanity of my characters. And now I empathize with my friend's father, who so many years ago did not have it so wrong; we need more bohemian postmodernist m*ther*ckers, but we also need more critics who challenge those mother*ckers' ideas.

Indeed, writers are interlocutors, but we are also travelers, exploring the open meadows of blank pages, navigating forward, trudging through deep-grass ideas, and plodding along the rocky trails word by word. We waltz, bop, and hopscotch across the bumpy page, stopping for a moment, lurching ahead with more precarious music, or seeking to silence sounds, stop them on a dime. Poets jump, shimmy, and pirouette. Fiction writers recline in the ample swath of white as if the story is a slow dream, or they speed through tunnels of allegory. No matter how a writer uses syntax and typography, we aim for our effects to work on the audience.

This is a story. This is a poem. This is an essay. A reader knows she is reading, sure. Still, she experiences something altogether different when she encounters an enjambed line or a white space, pausing in recognition so it shifts meaning and deepens the intention of a piece. I aim for the reader to lose herself or follow a line of dialogue so true to the characters that she listens as if she is eavesdropping behind a curtain in the room where the conversation occurs. Yes, writers manipulate words to make an impression, to create a deeper understanding, an empathy requiring engagement beyond a mere skim.

I travel through my memories and ideas to generate new fiction and poetry, but I am privileged to speak out on these pages. However, I am also limited by my perspective and what I have witnessed in this world; nonetheless, my

© CATE MCGOWAN, 2025 | DOI:10.1163/9789004712379_011

imperfect observations are the sharpest arrow in my craft quiver. In my frequent insecure moments, I ask myself, *What right do I have to speak for other women, or anyone, for that matter?* My answer is simple—I do not speak for anyone but myself. And maybe it is selfish, but it is all I have. I cannot appropriate someone's existence in the name of art.

My stories come from a deep belief in humanity's ability to set aside differences. I have worked to disregard a lifetime's accumulation of grievances and pettiness to appreciate better what makes people tick. The origins of my stories lie in a space of compassion and empathy, granting me the ability to imagine worlds I may never know. I have experienced both utter darkness and transcendent light; I have experienced an average life filled with struggle, injuries, and the limitations of rejection by a society that will never appreciate what I offer.

Initially, I came to my first foray into literary criticism, intending to show how certain forms of poetry might spur change. Poetry is a prime medium to express dissent and voice protest. As a scholar of World War I era literature, I know poetry's revolutionary potential is beyond doubt. Through my scholarship, I have witnessed how verse has historically been effective in critiquing social mores. In his "Preface to *The History of Sexuality*, Volume II" (1991), Foucault contends that a person's experiences are universal, historically trackable, and, thus, transformable if history is prologue. Therefore, a work of literature examined through Foucault's versatile lens might engage a person in their ordinary day-to-day moments through the specificity of language usage or narrative structure. In keeping with Foucault's perspective, engaging with literature might foster change and elicit interventions, leading to a shift in a person's immanence. Poetry might inspire people to detach from themselves and think in novel ways to create new realities.

Early in my studies, my poetics abandoned any alignment with Foucault's mission. As I have grown more cynical, I have become less convinced of how popular and avant-garde genres bring about lasting social change. The shock effects of any fresh or unconventional form might temporarily inspire innovative perspectives, but these innovative approaches or perceptions only result in extreme and rare departures from norms. Though concrete poetry and visual language use unconventional typography and unexpected metrical patterns, the styles are scarcely new or innovative. I have observed how poetic forms tending toward ephemerality or novelty are inevitably bound to appropriation by the status quo (a process Gertrude Stein sketches out in "Composition as Explanation," which she wrote in 1925).

Seamus Heaney, the Irish poet and Nobel Laureate, echoes my ambivalence. In 1988, at the height of Northern Ireland's Troubles, Heaney expressed his doubts about poetry's effectiveness in his essay "The Government of the Tongue." With a hollow yet resolute belief in poetry's "unlimited" worth, Heaney attempts to counter his grave concerns: "[T]he efficacy of poetry is nil—no lyric has ever stopped a tank" (1988, p. 107). Over sixty years before Heaney's pronouncements, Terry Eagleton relays an anecdote about how Marxist play-wright Bertolt Brecht had the same sentiment when mounting a production: "[He] remarked that putting a factory on stage would tell you nothing about the nature of capitalism" (2013, p. 68). Yes, I share Heaney's and Brecht's sus-picions about the inadequacies of attempting verisimilitude in literary and artistic pursuits. Representations of real life are *always* artificial constructions. Any consumer senses that the artwork they digest can never approximate or replace an actual real-world experience.

My doubts have pushed me toward short fiction studies, an endeavor more straightforward about its prevarications—fiction is not factual. But it can be true. The paradox appeals to me. While I believe in poetry's transforma-tive potential, stories incorporate reality and emotional truth without being disingenuous. An author composes fiction at the outset to be untrue, and a reader comes to the prose knowing it will be inaccurate. How an audience might actively listen necessitates the way stories are told. A narrative's seeds of wisdom do not demand explanations or justifications—an account is not ready-made. However, it is there to be absorbed, with each person's perspec-tive critical along a chain of comprehension.

People respond to stories more readily than other forms of information conveyance. Narration is how humans understand and interpret their worlds. Stories are not how-to manuals, but they allow an audience to integrate their feelings with the lessons of a story—a veritable condition of disbelief. Indeed, storytelling fosters cooperation, social cognition, and creativity. Human nature and storytelling exist within an evolutionary framework. And if one can avoid didacticism, telling a story creates cooperation.

Generating and innovating stories is a dynamic process, not a terminus but an adaptive route. Narratives inform readers about circumstances they will never experience firsthand. Readers can meet a stranger in a tale with whom they may never otherwise converse. Tales can make people feel for others and elicit empathy and active care for the populace. This care is the ultimate rev-olutionary act, for positive revolutionary improvements to the current state of affairs (patriarchy) are born out of concern for improving the conditions of others. Of course, I am presenting a romantic view of revolution—many uprisings have harmed the world significantly.

Knowledge of the human condition can compress and express itself in short stories, making them easily digestible and conveyable across the globe through print and digital media. People can translate these stories into other languages, reaching multitudes. This knowledge can only push the needle closer to com-passion. I, therefore, adhere to Hélène Cixous' appeals for women to write themselves—no matter the genre or form. Valie Export's groundbreaking words in "Women's Art" (1972) express my sentiments: "[L]et women speak so they can find themselves" (p. 1).

At my core, I am a Southern liberal woman who lives in a divided country refusing to reckon with its abhorrent racist past and present, a place barely coping with a never-ending pandemic and the equally pernicious epidemic of disinformation and eliminationist rhetoric enabling a growing sweep of global fascism. Another world war is a possibility. There is a threat to gay and trans-gender rights. American states are banning books. And those in power have stripped American women of bodily autonomy, relegating us again to the status of the "second sex."

•••

I am a product of what I read—I use authorial methods and techniques I absorb to improve my fictional creations and reveal the hardships of my artistic journey. Recently, I composed my own *Künstlerroman*, which I have set in the past. I am working on a new autofictional artist's novel set in contemporary times. In penning my stories, I write untrue tales with emotional sincerity. My process is thus paradoxical at its core. Literary creators and critics also embrace the idea that fiction reveals the world's stark actualities. For Rorty, in "Redemption from Egotism," the novel exposes readers to ways of thinking they may not confront in real life (2010, p. 393).

At the least, a fictional story's audience might encounter ideas they may not discover in philosophy or other scholarly nonfiction, allowing them to experience another human being's feelings. Because Freytagian story structures predicate conflict and resolve those problems, narrative readers immersed in a fictional character's travails might grow more empathetic and become engaged citizens when they suspend disbelief; however, change only happens if art and literature spur action. Literature is passive; it is the readers who are the change agents.

These days, as I continue to write, I ask challenging questions about problematic literature and criticism, including taking the critics to task who refuse to acknowledge a text's intentions or those who belittle innovative works. True art reflects social change and inspires new ways of conceptualizing established ideas. As I hone my scholarly and critical work, I ask three questions: How might literature encourage debates about harmful or sub-optimal conditions for those less privileged? How might my literature contribute to actionable dialogue without conveying artificial contrivances or evoking agenda-laden themes? How might my fiction foster empathy? I do not know how to answer these questions, but they are my practice's cornerstones.

At this moment in my scholarly pursuits, the modern world is too confound-ing for any discrete account to hold sway; I prefer to study the cultural influ-ences of many narrative styles to understand authorial choices; for example, many influential writers feature artists who come of age. I tackle this theme in all my narratives. The protagonist of my last novel, Jules Lalande, grows into an inspiring artist, but I had to move him around the narrative's game board so he could create. A need for creative fulfillment so whiplashes Lalande that he becomes a charlatan; he has no center, no self-identity, and he refuses to com-mit to anyone or any artistic outlet, bouncing from person to person, setting to setting. I hope readers relate to Lalande's ambivalence and psychic shapeshift-ing, his life reflecting our insecurities about our disordered world.

To relate to another person, real or fictional, can provide a route to under-standing and overcoming one's immanence. Fiction is about human nature *and* events, and infinite perspectives exist. Each story is unique, yet we all experience the same feelings. Thus, literature should not exist outside time, but within it and with no real beginnings or endings, like the Möbius strip in John Barth's *Funhouse*: "ONCE UPON A TIME THEREWAS A STORY THAT BEGAN" (2006, pp. 1–2).

The relentlessly threatening world confuses my attempts to understand rela-tionships, and my protective walls limit deep interaction with others. I use my point of view and platform to promote understanding. I trust readers. I hope. And yes, I aspire to inspire, promote more inclusive thinking, and express my truths. I can cede space in the world to carve out a place and invent anything I need here on the page.

References

Barth, J. (2006). *Lost in the funhouse: Fiction for print, tape, live voice*. Anchor Books.

Eagleton, T. (2013). *The gatekeeper: A memoir*. St. Martin's Press.

Export, V. (1972). *Women's art: A manifesto*. Monoskop.

Foucault, M. (1991). Preface to the history of sexuality, volume II. In P. Rabinow (Ed.), *The Foucault reader* (pp. 333–339). Penguin Books.

Heaney, S. (1988). The government of the tongue. In *The government of the tongue* (pp. 91–108). Faber and Faber.

Rorty, R. (2010). Redemption from egotism: James and Proust as spiritual exercises. In C. J. Voparil & R. J. Bernstein (Eds.), *The Rorty reader* (pp. 389–406). Wiley-Blackwell.

Stein, G. (1925). *Composition as explanation*. Retrieved March 23, 2024, from https://www.poetryfoundation.org/articles/69481/composition-as-explanation

Index

www.ingramcontent.com/pod-product-compliance
Lightning Source LLC
Chambersburg PA
CBHW021831020426
42334CB00014B/573